THE
MORAVIAN GRAVEYARDS
AT
NAZARETH, PA., 1744-1904

METALMARK BOOKS

The Moravian Graveyards

at Nazareth, Pa.,

1744-1904.

BY THE REV. EDW. T. KLUGE.

The Moravian Graveyards at Nazareth.

Comparatively few, who visit the graveyards of the Moravian Church at Nazareth, are aware, that in these beautifully located God's Acres many brethren and sisters have been laid to rest, who were prominent in the early history of the Church, whilst there are numbers of others, who, though never occupying positions entitling their names to be inscribed upon the annals of the Church, yet performed an important part in those first trying years of the Brethren's settlements in Pennsylvania. The names of many have been forgotten; the little stones, which marked their last resting place, have crumbled into dust; but in God's book of remembrance are treasured up their humble services, the sacrifices so willingly offered, the hardships endured, and, above all, the sterling Christian character of those first settlers, who labored, suffered and bore the heat and burden of those early days, not with any selfish object in view, not with the hope of accumulating wealth, or even a home of their own, but only to perform their part in establishing the Church in the wilds of the new world, and for the glory of God and the spread of His gospel of grace.

THE ANNOUNCEMENT OF DEATHS.

While in many churches the death of a member is made known by tolling of the church-bell, (the number of strokes of the bell indicating the number of years of the departed,) the old Moravian custom of making the announcement is by means of the solemn strains of the trombones from the steeple of the church. Formerly everyone was familiar both with the hymns and the melodies or tunes of the Church, and, as many of the latter were associated with a well-known hymn, there was no difficulty experienced in recognizing the significance of an announcement from the steeple of the church. This being no longer the case, the beauty and impressiveness of this custom, as well as the significance of the tunes by the trombonists in the early hours of a festival day, have, in a great measure, been lost. Believing that a list of the tunes used for the announcement of deaths may be appreciated by many, we here append the same. The first tune is 151A, which is to remind us of an old German hymn, which announces, in beautiful language, that a fellow-pilgrim has been called home: "Es schied aus unserm Bunde, Ein Pilgrim uns voran," etc. The second one indicates from which division or class of the congregation a soul has departed:

For Married Men, Tune 83. "Jesus ne'er forsaketh me, This my spirit greatly cheereth; And my constant trust shall be; Yea, though death at length appeareth; Herein precious comfort lies; I shall in His image rise."

For Married Women, Tune 79. "His plea amid deep sighing, With bitter tears and crying, My soul with peace doth bless," etc.

For Widowers, Tune 132A. "Therefore my hope is in His grace, And not in my own merit; On Him my confidence I place," etc.

For Widows, Tune 149. "Oh, what happiness divine, Oh, the lot most precious," etc.

For Unmarried Men, Tune 185. "Faithful Lord, my only joy and treasure," etc.

For Unmarried Women, Tune 37. "My happy lot is here the Lamb to follow," etc.

For Older Boys, Tune 23. "With new grace, dear Lord, array me," etc.

For Older Girls, Tune 14A. "Oh, that I may so favored be With them above to join;" etc.

For Little Boys, Tune 39. "We thank Thee, that Thou wilt the children permit," etc.

For Little Girls, Tune 82. "Should not I for gladness leap, Led by Jesus as His sheep," etc.

The third tune is the same as the first one, viz. 151A, the hymn associated with this melody being a prayer, in view of our own departure: viz., "Be near *me* when *I'm* dying, Oh, show Thy cross to me!" etc.

The plaintive tones of these sweet melodies have touched hearts, spoken to souls, breathed comfort, peace, hope into many an one, and raised thoughts far above earth to heaven and the coming glory. On the occasion of a funeral, the tune, indicating the division of the congregation from which the departed has been called home, is generally performed on entering the graveyard.

The Moravians regarded the congregation as a *large family ;* all were brethren and sisters; and this idea was not disregarded when the departed were laid to rest on their God's Acres. No distinction is made between the wealthy and the poor, the learned and illiterate, the honored and the humblest of God's children. The brethren are interred in one plot, the sisters in another; the children in a space allotted to them, etc. A simple slab of marble marks their resting places. There is a deep significance in the customs of our forefathers, though not always appreciated by all.

THE FIRST GRAVEYARD.

The first graveyard of the Nazareth settlement was consecrated on the occasion of the burial of George Kremser, on Jan. 18, 1744. The service was a brief one, on that cold winter's day, and amid the dangers which often threatened the Brethren on funeral occasions; for we are told, that it was frequently deemed prudent for some of the Brethren to be armed, on account of possible attacks from hostile Indians.

This graveyard is located on the highest point in this section of the country, and was selected by Captain N. Garrison, the well-known sea-captain and surveyor, not only on account of the fact just stated, but probably also as being convenient for the settlements of Gnadenthal, Christian's Spring, Old Nazareth, Friedensthal and the "Rose."

It is difficult to account for the strange misnomer, "the Indian Graveyard," which, in modern times, has been given to this spot. Only four Indians are buried here, viz.: Salome, an Indian woman; Maria Spangenberg, the daughter of Ruth, an Indian from Shekomeko, who was baptized at Bethlehem, May 13, 1746; Sarah, daughter of the Indian Nathaniel, a child from the school, baptized by Brother Christian Henry Rauch, and Beata, daughter of the Indian Philip, who died five days after her baptism.

The designations given by the Brethren to this graveyard were Ruheberg (the hill of rest), Hutberg, after the graveyard at Herrnhut, and the more common name, Gottesacker, or God's Acre.

The first graveyard at Nazareth is beautifully located, the land-scape from this elevation being most picturesque, the Blue Mountains, like a mighty wall, limiting the view to the north, while to the south and east is spread out the country lying between Nazareth and Bethlehem, little villages and hamlets dotting the landscape, with the South Mountain in the back-ground.

It was a matter of deep regret that this beautiful and sacred spot passed out of the possession of the Church at the time when the extensive farms and woodland belonging to and constituting Gnadenthal, were sold to the County for the establishment of the Almshouse, and Christian's Spring and land, lying between that quaint little hamlet and Nazareth, to private individuals. This occurred about sixty years ago, the Brethren at Nazareth being filled with indignation and vainly protesting. The graveyard was included in the sale, the only condition being that the ground of this little plot should not be tilled. At that time the mounds of the graves were in a tolerable condition, covered with thyme and the beautiful mountain-pink, and the larger portion of the modest little tombstones were still in position and legible. The owner of the property, faithful to the conditions made in the deed, did not plough nor sow the graveyard, but, if possible, con-signed the sacred spot to a more ignoble use, making it the dump-ing-place for the large quantity of quartz stones and rubbish gathered from his land. Nazareth appears to have been power-less to prevent the desecration of this first God's Acre.

Finally, after many years and great difficulties, the plot was secured by the joint action of the Moravian Historical Society (soon after its organization), and the Board of Trustees of the church at Nazareth. It was purchased from Mr. Abraham Gruver, who had become the owner, for the sum of $150—a very large sum for so small a piece of ground in those days; and from Mr. Edwin P. Wolle and others a strip of land for an approach to the graveyard, at the rate of $125 an acre. The Trustees of Nazareth church hold the deed, the Historical Society having later received a perpetual lease.

It was no trifling undertaking to reclaim and restore this waste place to a condition worthy of the object for which it had been dedicated in 1744, as the Historical Society at that time had only a small membership and was almost without means. The ground was cleared, the few remnants of tombstones removed to the museum of the Society, and a monument, prepared by Mr. Robert Haas of Nazareth, was erected, while Mr. John Jordan had a small pavilion (a reminder of the one on the Hutberg at Herrnhut), built at his own expense, the property being enclosed by a fence and some trees planted on the graveyard and the walk to this sacred spot.

On the 12th of June, 1867, the formal unveiling of the monument and the re-dedication of the graveyard took place. A large number of members and friends of the Church from Bethlehem, Philadelphia, New York, Brooklyn, Lititz, Schoeneck and Nazareth had assembled. The trombonists from Schoeneck and Nazareth furnished music, alternating with one another, as the large procession wended its way up the hills to the graveyard. The Nazareth church choir attended in a body, and in addition to leading the singing of hymns by the congregation, sang a pretty anthem, composed for the occasion by Brother Benjamin Clewell, the organist of the church at Nazareth. The burial litany was prayed by the Rev. Robert de Schweinitz, Principal of Nazareth Hall, and two addresses were made, the one by the Rev. Edward Rondthaler, pastor of the church in Brooklyn, and the other by the Rev. E. T. Kluge, pastor of the church at Nazareth. Bishop J. C. Jacobson, President of the Provincial Elders' Conference, pronounced the benediction.

On the monument are inscribed the names of those interred in this graveyard. The monument is made of American marble, the total cost being $448.30. Sixty-seven persons are here interred, viz., fifty-two children, eleven white adults, and four Indians, two of whom are children.

As this graveyard was in use upwards of twelve years, the number of adult members buried here is small, especially if the fact is borne in mind, that those first settlers were subjected to many hardships and discomforts, and that, during these years, contagious diseases—amongst the rest, the small-pox—prevailed. The large number of little children who died, is easily accounted for. By far the larger number had lived in the nursery at Ephrata; for, on account of the peculiar conditions existing at that time, parents were obliged to place their little children in the nursery, so that they might receive the care and attention, which it was impossible for them to bestow, as the large majority in Bethlehem, Nazareth, and other settlements were occupied in felling the forests, preparing the land for tillage, and carrying on the various pursuits begun in the colonies, the women also being occupied in many ways. Besides, the homes prepared for the large numbers, who were constantly coming here from Europe and England, as well as from various sections of this country, were insufficient for their proper accommodation.

Of the names of families represented among those interred in this first graveyard, very few are now to be found in the Church. The names which occur, which are familiar, are the following : Samuel Krause, Andrew Kremser, Jacob Till, Clewell, Demuth, Christ, together with Michler, descendants still living in Easton, Büninger, (later spelled Bininger,) descendants having formerly been prominent members of the Church in New York, and some still living in that city; Mücke, descendants living in Lititz, Pa.

Of the adult members buried here, there are several, who deserve particular notice :

CHRISTOPH DEMUTH, a manufacturer of paper-boxes, came from Moravia. In 1726, being greatly troubled in spirit and longing for peace, he forsook his home, and by a wonderful leading of Providence, came to Herrnhut. Apparently he had not decided where to go, nor had he heard anything of Count Zinzendorf, nor of the refuge there offered by him for refugees from Moravia. A few weeks later he returned to Moravia for his wife and two children. Brother Demuth was present at the communion at Berthelsdorf, on August 13, 1727, and was a participant. In 1726, in company with Christian David, he went to Moravia, remaining there six months; and, although in danger of imprisonment, visited devout souls in various places, who, in their concealment, were longing for freedom to worship the Lord according to the dictates of their consciences and to enjoy the spiritual blessings which their fathers of the Brethren's Church had so highly prized. Living in Herrnhut, and supporting himself by the labor of his hands, he made many journeys in the cause of the Lord. Amongst the rest, he went to Berlin in 1729, to various portions of Prussia in 1732, in company with

Frederick Boehnisch, to Würtemberg in 1730, in order to accompany two young women from Switzerland to Herrnhut. In 1743, together with 120 others, he and his family came to Pennsylvania, later serving in Mülhbach, Germantown, and Fredericktown as minister. He was an excellent singer, and when preaching to the people, he often proclaimed the gospel in song, which was very edifying and impressive, as was also his devout walk ("priesterlicher Wandel"). During the greater part of the time, Nazareth was his home, where "his example of holy living was not without blessed fruits." On the last day of his life, though with a feeble voice, he frequently repeated his favorite hymn, "Jesu Kreuze, Jesu Todesstunden, Jesu, über alles schöne Wunden, Jesu, Gottes-Leichelein, Soll mein Ein und Alles sein." Two of his children survived him: Ferdinand, and a daughter, married to Peter Thiel. His age was 64 years, 3 months and 20 days.

JOHANNES MUENSTER, one of the first exiles from Moravia and members of the Herrnhut congregation. He was born in Zauchtenthal in 1700. In the great awakening in Moravia, he was deeply impressed, and, in consequence, came to Herrnhut in 1725. He too was a participant in the memorable communion on August 13th, 1727. In the service of the congregation, he was commissioned to make visits to various parts of the country, in one of which he became acquainted with the Dober family, which figures so prominently in early Moravian history. Twice he went to Moravia, the last time bringing with him his mother and three of his brothers and sisters. He was married to a daughter of Brother Nitschmann. In 1742, during the war between Prussia and Austria, he was twice sent, with his wife, to Silesia, where they labored with blessing among awakened souls in that country. He and his family came to Pennsylvania with the "Second Sea Congregation," among the so-called "Fischer Gesellschaft." In this country he served in various capacities, in Oley, Skippack, Muddy Creek, Macungie, Bethlehem, Friedensthal and Nazareth.

Others, deserving special mention, are the following:

ELIZABETH TILL, m.n. Stephan, wife of Jacob Till, was born in Switzerland. At her urgent request, her father took her to

Herrnhaag, when quite young, as she "longed to be the Lord's property and to serve Him." This she did in Gnadeck, Herrnhut, Marienborn, Zeist, Herrndyk, generally in Children's Homes. Together with a large company, she came to this country in 1753, on the ship *Irene*, and here rendered valuable services.

ELIZABETH PAYNE, mother of the Rev. Jasper Payne, a minister of the church. She was born in England in 1669. Through her son she became acquainted with the Brethren and united with the Church. In 1743, although in her 74th year, she came to this country, with her son and 120 others, in the vessel *Little Strength*. On the voyage she was of much service to the English Brethren and Sisters of the company; and during her stay in Bethlehem, was very helpful to missionaries and others. When no longer able to serve others, on account of her age and infirmities, she prayed for them. She died in Nazareth in the 87th year of her life, her death being the first which occurred in the Widows' House.

ANNA MARGARETHA NILSON, m.n. Henckel ,was another valued woman, who came to this country, as a member of one of the "sea-congregations."

Two others, CATHARINE HILLMAN, m. n. Kaiser, and ARIANCHY COUNTRYMAN, her sister, the wife of Henry Countryman, both from England, should also be mentioned. They became acquainted with Brother Burnside, while on their way to Virginia, and were so deeply impressed by the preaching of the Brethren, that they decided to abandon the idea of moving to Virginia and remained in Dansbury (in what is now Monroe County), in order to be under the spiritual care of the Moravian Brethren. The Indians having threatened the place, all fled, taking refuge in Nazareth. Here, after a stay of only a few weeks, both died on the same day, probably from the effects of their flight.

JOHANN BAUMAN, a married man, whose father was a Mennonite in Conestoga, is also buried here. He had been baptized by the Mennonites; but, having been deeply impressed by the teaching of the Brethren, his father bought land, about five miles from Gnadenthal, upon which the young man and his wife were to live so that they might be near the Brethren, "because his son loved them so dearly." Young Bauman was shot and scalped by the Indians. His father brought the remains to Gnadenthal, with the request that his son might be laid to rest with those whom he loved and who had been so great a blessing to him.

Although the number of persons interred on the first graveyard is very small, only 67, of whom 52 are children, 11 white adults, and 4 Indians, two of whom were children,—the spot is worthy of being held sacred; the few to whom reference has been made being pious men and women, who contributed, in no small degree, to the work of the Church, and whose lives preached eloquently to many, both in Europe and this country, of the love and grace of the Saviour; men who belonged to the number who forsook home and kindred for the sake of the gospel, and who link us to the Ancient Church of the Brethren. The few Indians, first fruits of missionary labor in this part of the country, and the large number of little children, whose early death speak loudly of the privations and sacrifices made by the first Christian settlers of this portion of Pennsylvania; they also add to the sacredness of this spot. Surely it is Holy Ground; the "Ruheberg," the resting place of many wearied followers of the Saviour.

COMPLETE LIST OF THOSE INTERRED ON THE FIRST GRAVEYARD.

1744.
Jan. 18. **George Kremser**, married man. Born in Silesia.
Apr. 16. **Elizabeth Hanke**, m. n. Henckel, wife of Matthew Hanke. Born in Wetteravia.

1745.
Feb. 25. **Thomas Adolph Schaaf**, a child.

1746.
Jan. 2. **John Michler**, infant son of John and Barbara Michler.
Feb. 4. **Christian Fritsche**, child.
Apr. 30. **Anna Maria Klotz**, married woman, wife of Ludwig Klotz, of Bethlehem.
Aug. 12. **Rebecca Burnside**, daughter of James Burnside. Died in the nursery.
Aug. 19. **Beata**, daughter of the Indian **Philip**. 5 years old. Nursery.
Aug. 22. **Sarah**, daughter of the Indian **Nathaniel**. 6 years old. Nursery. Funeral held by Brother Christian Henry Rauch.
Aug. 29. **Nathaniel Grabs**, son of John and Anna M. Grabs.
Nov. 19. **Maria Bresier** (Brashier).

1747.
Aug. 15. **John Klotz**, infant son of Albrecht and Marg. Klotz.
Sept. 16. **Maria Michler**, infant daughter of John and Barbara Michler.

1748.
Jan. 14. **Anna Elizabeth Kohn**, child from the nursery.
Jan. 18. **David Reichard,** ⎞ Children from the nursery. Both buried at the
Jan. 20. **Anna Fritsche,** ⎠ same time.
Mar. 27. **Maria Spangenberg,** an Indian from Shekomeko. Daughter of Ruth. Baptized May 13, 1746, at Bethlehem. Aged 11 years. A pupil in the school.
Dec. 21. **Salome,** an Indian woman.

1749.
Mar. 6. **Beata Boehmer.**
Mar. 12. **John Michael Muecke,** son of Michael and Cath. Muecke. Died in the nursery.
Apr. 17. **Joseph Hussey,** child from nursery.
Aug. 5. **Sophia Jarvis,** child from nursery.

1750.
Mar. 18. **Johanna Schaefer,** infant daughter of John Nicholas and Johanna Schaefer. The first death in Gnadenthal.

1751.
Jan. 23. **Joseph Schneider,** infant son of Adam and Eliz. Schneider. Died in the nursery.
Feb. 7. **Anna Margaretha Nilson,** m.n. Henckel. Born in Langen Diebach, near Hanau. Awakened in Herrnhaag, 1741. 1743 married Jonas Nilson, at the same time with thirty other couples, destined for Pennsylvania, and who formed part of one of the "sea congregations." Aged 30 years.
Feb. 12. **Gottfried Grabs,** child of John G. and Anna M. Grabs.
Mar. 17. **Anna Maria Grabs,** sister of the foregoing. Both from nursery.
April 2. **Samuel Krause,** infant son of Samuel and Rosina Krause.
May 9. **Anna Maria Jorde,** infant daughter of John and Mary Jorde.
June 1. **Ludwig Enerson,** infant son of Ebert and Marg. Enerson.
June 19. **Elizabeth Werner,** married woman, m.n. Blum, from Gnadenthal.

1752.
Jan. 27. **Johannes Reichardt,** son of David and Elizabeth Reichardt. Born in Fredericktown, April 22, 1750.
Feb. 20. **Anna Maria Biefel,** child from the nursery.
Feb. 6. **Julianna Schmidt,** daughter of John and Dorothea Schmidt. Nursery.
Mar. 29. **Benigna Roseen,** daughter of the Rev. Sven and A. M. Roseen. Nursery.
Apr. 13. **Elizabeth Mueller,** daughter of J. H. and Rosina Mueller of Bethlehem. Died in nursery
Apr. 16. **Paulus and Petrus Fritsche,** twin children of Paul and Rosina Fritsche.
May 14. **Johannes Stoll,** son of John and Mary Stoll, Friedensthal. Nursery.
Sept. 30. **Anna Schneider,** daughter of John and Elizabeth Schneider, Gnadenthal. Nursery. "Wurde in der Nursery heimgeküsst."
Oct. 25. **Johannes Kremser,** son of Andreas and Rosina Kremser, Fredericktown. Nursery.
Nov. 17. **Beata Anderson,** daughter of Gottlieb and Christina Anderson. Nursery.
(Eleven children in one year.)

1753.

May 19. **Beatus Schulze,** son of Gottfried Schulze, Gnadenthal.

June 14. **John David Michler,** infant son of Wolfgang and Rosina Michler.

Oct. 1. **Anna Elizabeth Goetje.**

1754.

Jan. 26. **Margaretha Christ,** daughter of Rudolph and Anna Christ, Gnadenthal. Born in Würtemberg.

Jan. 28. **Paulus Fritsche,** son of Paul and Rosina Fritsche. "Kehrte bald wieder zu seiner Mutterstadt."

Mar. 5. **Christoph Demuth,** born in Cathelsdorf, Moravia. Aged 64 years, 3 months and 20 days.

April 2. **Martha Bueninger,** infant daughter of Abraham and Martha Bueninger. Nursery.

May 30. **Johannes Muenster,** one of the first exiles from Moravia. Aged 54 years.

Aug. 21. **John Henry Moeller,** son of John Henry and Rosina Moeller. Nursery.

Sept. 2. **Elizabeth Hafner.** Nursery.

Sept. 17. **Magdalena Mordick,** Gnadenhütten on the Mahoney. Nursery.

Sept. 18. **Anna Maria Engel,** from York. Nursery.

Oct. 22. **Elizabeth Till,** m.n. Stephan. Born in Mühlhausen, Switzerland, March 28, 1724. One of the members of the "Sea Congregation" in 1753. A highly valued attendant in the nursery; motherly and kind.

1755.

June 5. **Elizabeth Payne,** m.n. Banister. Born in England, April 26, 1669,— the oldest member in this country. Mother of Jasper Payne. Came to this country in the *Little Strength*, as one of the "Sea Congregation." Aged 87.

Sept. 15. **Louisa Partsch,** daughter of George and Louisa Partsch.

Dec. 2. **Beata Mueller,** daughter of Joseph and Verona Müller.

1756.

Jan. 20. **Johann Bauman.** Born in Conestoga, 1727. Shot and scalped by the Indians.

Feb. 1. **Arianchy Countryman,** m.n. Kaiser, sister of Mrs. Hillman and wife of Henry Countryman. Died on the same day as her sister.

Feb. 1. **Catharine Hillman,** m.n. Kaiser, wife of John Hillman, from England. Both she and her sister were refugees on the occasion of Indian troubles in Dansbury, now in Monroe County. Died seven weeks after reaching Nazareth. She had 13 children. Aged 42.

Feb. 29. **Samuel Hillman.**

May 6. **Sarah Culver,** daughter of Ephraim Culver.

Sept. 11. **Anna Maria Opitz,** daughter of Leopold Opitz. 12 years old. Died in consequence of the bite of a snake.

1757.

July 5. **Susanna Wickel,** adopted daughter of George Volk of Allemängel; 15 years old. Died at the Rose Inn.

1760.

Oct. 23. **Nathaniel Clewell,** infant son of Franz Clewell, Plainfield.

1762.

May 8. **Abraham Clewell,** infant son of George Clewell, Plainfield.

THE SECOND GRAVEYARD.

The second graveyard, now in use, was opened on the 14th of February, 1756, on the occasion of the funeral of John Peter Lehnert or Lennert, "das erste Waizenkorn auf diesem Gottesacker." Bishop Spangenberg held the funeral and consecrated the ground, delivering a brief address on the words, "But I am a worm, and no man." Psalm 22 : 6.

A beautiful location had again been selected on the hill overlooking a wide expanse of country, bounded by mountains. During many years every effort to improve and beautify this spot proved fruitless. It appeared to be a rather barren spot. Two lone linden trees, which never attained any considerable size were the only ones in the enclosure at the gateway, while the graves were covered with the aromatic thyme and mountain pinks, the only plants which appeared to thrive. At the entrance on the east side, there was a neat gateway, with an arch, containing two inscriptions ; the one on the east side, a German one, "Ich lebe, und Ihr sollt auch leben ;" on the west side, an English one, "The body rests in hope."

About sixty years ago, efforts were made by the late Brethren John Beitel, Sr., Christian Brunner and others to plant trees. Having repeatedly failed, they finally conveyed to the spot large trees in the depth of winter, carefully dug up with an abundance of frozen soil, hoping thus to succeed ; but in vain ; and after many disappointments and most persevering labor, extending over many years, the plan was abandoned ; for nothing would grow on this place of the dead ! Later, about forty-five or more years ago, another effort was made by the late Brethren Edmund Ricksecker, Dr. Charles Sellers, William Christ and others ; and this met with success. A large variety of trees, especially evergreens, were successfully planted ; and it is maintained by those capable of judging correctly, that the collection of evergreens was the largest and most complete in any portion of the State, many being extremely rare. Since then many changes have taken place, and the axe has been freely used. No doubt, much of this was necessary ; but, in all probability, the large variety of interesting deciduous and evergreen trees was not known to those who wielded the axe, nor the labors and troubles of the good men, who now sleep their last sleep in this sacred spot, which they had endeavored to beautify.

In this graveyard are interred the remains of upwards of forty-five ministers, missionaries and wives of ministers, some of whom had held prominent positions in the Church and rendered valuable services. A number of former Nazareth pastors rest here with the members of their flock; amongst these *Franz Christian Lembke*, who served as pastor in Nazareth nearly thirty years, and also, for some years as principal of Nazareth Hall and a member of the Provincial Board. Amongst other prominent people buried here, are a number, who were born in Zauchtenthal and other places in Moravia and Bohemia, some of whom had belonged to the company of exiles from the original home of the Brethren's Church and first members of the Renewed Church, and had participated in the ever memorable communion at Berthelsdorf, August 13th, 1727; also many of the ancestors of the Moravians of the present day; noted physicians, such as Dr. John Frederick Otto, Joseph Otto, Stephen Bruce, Henry Schmidt, besides highly gifted and respected physicians of later times. Besides, there are a number of negroes, for many years slaves, who had been captured in Guinea and brought to this country; and also refugees from Wyoming and other places, Nazareth being a haven of rest and safety to a large number.

The total number here interred is 1134.

In the following list of burials in the second, or present, graveyard, the names are printed and numbered in the order of interment. The characters following each name indicate the location of the grave, and these are followed by the date of decease. The rows of graves are indicated by Roman numerals counting from the East, those to the North of the middle path being designated by the letter n, and those to the South by the letter s. The Arabic numerals denote the number of each grave counting from the middle walk, thus:

1. John Peter Lehnert. ix, s. 1. Feb. 14, 1756,

signifies that the first interment was that of John Peter Lehnert who was buried in the ninth row, and the first grave south of the middle walk, and that his death occurred on the 14th of February, 1756.

1756.

1. **John Peter Lehnert,** (Lennert). ix, s. 1. Feb. 14. Born in Freyrachdorf, Dürdorf, June 2, 1721, his parents being members of the Reformed Church. In 1740, Oct. 18, he came to Philadelphia, where he was awakened by a sermon preached by Zinzendorf, on Easter, 1742. Removed to Bethlehem in 1743, and united with the congregation. 1747 married to Anna Brock. He was employed in the schools at Bethlehem, Nazareth and Magunschi (Emmaus) and later on the farms in Gnadenthal. His age was 33 years, 7 months and 9 days.

2. **Anna Dorothea Grabs.** iv, n. 1. June 22. A child in the nursery, aged 3 years. Daughter of Gottfried and Maria Grabs of Bethlehem.

1757.

3. **Charlotte Sophia Richter.** iv, n. 2. Mar. 8. A child in the nursery, aged 3 years. Daughter of J. Christian and Charlotte Richter of Bethlehem.

4. **Gertrude Sehner.** iv, n. 3. Mar. 29. A child, aged 1 year and 9 months. Daughter of Peter Sehner of Bethlehem.

5. **Infant.** vi, s. 1. Apr. 27. Infant of Henry and Anna Maria Frey.

6. **Maria Eva Birstler,** m.n. Roth. viii, n. 1. July 17. Born in Gerstdorf in Alsace, Aug. 29, 1729. Aged 27 years.

7. **Christian Thomas Benzien.** ix, s. 2. Aug. 4. "Liturgus" in Gnadenthal. Aged 42 years.

8. **Joseph Frey.** vi. s. 2. Aug. 23. An infant.

9. **Jens. Kolkier.** ii, s. 1. Sept. 12. The first unmarried man, belonging to the Brethren's Choir in Christianspring, who departed this life.

10. **John Birstler.** vi, s. 3. Oct. 24. A small child.

1758.

11. **Michael Muenster.** ii, s. 2. March 8. An unmarried man; a carpenter from Moravia, who came to Nazareth, in order to work at the erection of the Hall.

12. **Philip Wesa.** ix, s. 3. Mar. 18. Lost his life in an accident which occurred between the "Rose Inn" and Nazareth. His horses having run away, he was crushed by the wagon. "Seine morsche Hütte wurde in die Erde zur Cur und Rectification gelegt."

13. **Margaretha Gloz.** viii, n. 2. June 13. A married woman; her infant was buried in the same grave.

14. **Anna Zeisberger,** m.n. Boehm. viii, n. 3. July 16. Second wife of George Zeisberger of Gnadenthal. She was born in Kunewalde, in Moravia, and was married in Herrnhut. Her husband having been called to America, they came to Bethlehem in 1743; later removed to Gnadenthal, where Brother Zeisberger superintended the clearing of the land and establishing of the farms. Aged 58 years.

15. **Paul.** ix, s. 4. July 18. An Indian, living in Gnadenthal. Baptized during his last illness in Gnadenthal.

16. **Daniel Fritsch.** vi, s. 4. Sept. 17. A child.

17. **Catharine Helena Fritsch.** viii, n. 4. Sept 26. The mother of Daniel Fritsch.

1759.

18. **Joseph Jorde.** vi, s. 5. Aug. 2. A pupil in Nazareth Hall.
19. **John Peter Braun.** vi, s. 6. Aug. 23. A child from the nursery.
20. **John Henry Mueller.** vi, s. 7. Sept. 19. A child from the nursery.

1760.

21. **Elizabeth Merck.** viii, n. 5. Feb. 23. Wife of Henry Merck.
22. **Gottlieb Anders.** ii, s. 3. May 21. A child.
23. **John Michael Enerson.** vi, s. 8. June 7. A child.
24. **Anna Catharine Moeller.** iv, n. 4. July 6. A child.
25. **John Frederick Kunkler.** vii, s. 1. July 22. A child ten years old.
26. **John Henry Richling.** ii, s. 4. July 30. Unmarried man.
27. **John Frederick Beyer.** ix, s. 5. Aug. 11.
28. **Conrad Okertshausen.** ix, s. 6. Aug. 26.
29. **Sophia Barbara Steup.** viii, n. 6. Sept. 9.
30. **John Francis Steup.** vii, s. 2. Sept. 29. Child from the nursery.

1761.

31. **Joseph Mueller.** ix, s. 7. Feb. 20. Married man.
32. **Anna Maria Demuth.** viii, n. 7. March 1. Widow.
33. **Joshua.** ii, s. 5. May 11. A negro, who died of small-pox at Christianspring.
34. **Christian Flex.** vii, s. 3. May 17. Child, Gnadenthal.
35. **John Frederick Wittke.** vii, s. 4. May 29. Child, died of small-pox.
36. **John Frederick Schaub.** vii, s. 5. May 30. Child, died of small-pox.
37. **Christian Gottlieb Hussey.** vii, s. 6. June 2. Child, died of small-pox.
38. **Martin Nitschmann.** vii, s. 7. June 3. Child, died of small-pox. His father was killed at Gnadenhütten on the Mahony, at the fearful massacre.
39. **Immanuel Goetje.** vii, s. 8. June 4. Child, died of small-pox.
40. **John Martin Shebosh.** iv, s. 1. June 5. Child, died of small-pox.
41. **Gottlieb Moeller.** iv, s. 2. June 7. Child, died of small-pox.
42. **David Ludwig Fritsch.** iv, s. 3. June 12. Child, died of small-pox.
43. **Matthew Wittke.** ix, s. 8. June 19. Married man, Christianspring.
44. **John Michael Graff.** iv, s. 4. July 8. Child from nursery.
45. **Christian Fritsch.** iv, s. 5. July 14. Child from the nursery.
   (Of the children, whose deaths are recorded during 1761, nearly all died of small-pox, that disease prevailing particularly in the nursery.)
46. **Catharine.** viii, n. 8. Nov. 8. A negro, a widow in Gnadenthal.

1762.

47. **Anna Maria Birstler.** iv, n. 5. April 6. Infant daughter of John and Anna M. Birstler.
48. **Anna Margaret Enerson,** m. n. Drews. ix, n. 1. April 27. Born on the island of Riga, Dec. 19, 1719. In 1742 she came to Herrnhut, where she united with the congregation. 1749 came to Bethlehem, together with many others, with Brother John Nitschmann, and was married to Enert Enerson.
49. **Beatus Weinert.** iv, s. 6. May 9.
50. **Gottfried Schwarz.** ii, s. 6. June 14. An unmarried man from Christians-spring. Born in Denckendorf, Würtemberg. While serving as a soldier he was awakened. Together with eleven other soldiers he went to Herrnhaag,

2

after he had received his discharge from the army, and was received into the congregation. In 1750, together with 84 unmarried brethren, he came to Bethlehem with Brother Jorde. Later removed to Christianspring. Aged 52.

51. **Regina Hantsch.** ix, n. 2. June 27. A widow. Born 1688 in Ottendorf. Married, 1714, to George Hantsch. In 1739 she followed her children to Herrnhut, where she and her husband were received into the congregation. In 1743 she and her husband and two children, George and Regina, came to Bethlehem. These formed a little company of Christian "pilgrims," and travelled through the country endeavoring to do good. In 1749 she was received as an acolyte. After the death of her husband in 1754, she removed to the Widows' House.

1763.

52. **Christian Fredr. Otto.** iv, s. 7. Jan. 24. Son of Matthew and Sophia Otto, of Bethlehem. Died in Nazareth Hall, aged 8 years.

53. **Rudolph Christ.** viii, s. 1. May 22. Born in Lauffen, Würtemberg, May 23, 1710. Baptized in Lutheran Church. 1733, July 21, married Anna Wolfer. Having been awakened in 1744, he visited in Herrnhaag repeatedly. In 1750 moved to this country, with his wife and six children, and lived in Bethlehem. In 1755 united with the congregation.

54. **Anna Maria Christ, m.n.** Schroller. ix, n. 3. June 25. Born in Gottsdorf, in Upper Silesia, March 25, 1703. Her parents were members of the Lutheran Church. In her twentieth year she became acquainted with the Brethren and was led to the Saviour. In 1736 she removed to Herrnhut and later was received into the congregation. In 1743 married George Christ in Marienborn, and came to this country with a large number of colonists, living at first in Bethlehem; later in Nazareth.

55. **David Segner.** iv, s. 8. Dec. 10. Son of John Henry and Christine (Frey) Segner. Aged 6 years.

56. **Christine Catharine Berndt.** iv, n. 6. Dec. 13. An infant. "Kehrte in ihre Mutterstadt zurück."

57. **Anna Eva Meyer.** ix, n. 4. Dec. 17. A widow. Born in 1688 in Würtemberg. Having moved to England, she was awakened by the preaching of Whitefield, and later became acquainted with Bishop Spangenberg, and united with the Brethren's Church. In 1749 she came to Bethlehem as a widow, and in 1755, together with the entire "choir" of widows, removed to Nazareth. "Bewiess sich als ein attachirtes Herz an den Martermann und Sein Volk."

1764.

58. **Daniel Sehner.** iii, s. 1. Jan. 12. Infant son of Peter Sehner.

59. **Beatus Mueller.** iii, s. 2. June 5. Infant son of Henry Mueller.

60. **Christian Moeller.** iii, s. 3. Nov. 10. Infant son of Joseph Moeller.

1765.

61. **Susanna Somers.** ix, n. 5. March 14. A widow. Born in England, near Cambridge, April 5, 1695. Baptized in the Episcopal Church. Married Balthaser Somers of Frankfort-on-the-Main and moved to Amsterdam. 1752 to New York, her husband having died. There she united with the Brethren's Church. Later moved to Bethlehem and finally to Nazareth.

62. **Anna Elizabeth Leinbach,** m.n. Kleiz. ix, n. 6. April 25. Born in Germany in 1680. In 1700 married John Leinbach, a teacher and organist. In 1723, the family came to this country, settling in Oley, Pennsylvania. Bishop Spangenberg visited the family, as did also Count Zinzendorf and Sister Molther, who were instrumental in leading them to Christ. She was received into the congregation at Bethlehem, continuing to live in Oley. Her husband having died in 1747, she removed to Bethlehem a few years later, and then to Nazareth. Three sons and two daughters survived.

63. **Paul Fritsche.** viii, s. 2. Nov. 10. He was born in Zauchtenthal, Moravia, Jan. 6, 1722. His parents were members of the Brethren's Church. Hearing the gospel from Brethren who came to Moravia from Herrnhut, he was deeply impressed, and removing to Herrnhut, united with the congregation. In 1749, came to America with a large number of colonists, living for some time in Bethlehem, where he married Rosina Hans. Later he removed to Nazareth and Friedensthal.

1766.

64. **Martin Liebisch.** viii, s. 3. Feb. 1. Born in Zauchtenthal, Moravia, in Nov. 1698. His parents were descendants of the Brethren. In 1722, he married Anna Schneider. Of his seven children, three survived their father, viz: Samuel in Herrnhut, David in the East Indies, and an unmarried daughter, Joanna, in Bethlehem. In 1730 he came to Herrnhut and united with the congregation. There he superintended the orphan-school. In 1742 he was called to this country, where he labored faithfully in Bethlehem, Fredericks-town, Nazareth, Gnadenthal and Christianspring. His age was 67. A large number of emigrants from Moravia, as also Brother and Sister David Nitschmann, (on a visit from Europe) and the aged Bishop David Nitsch-mann, came from Bethlehem to attend his funeral.

65. **Anna Catharine Flex,** m.n. Renner. ix, n. 7. April 19. Born March 17,1717, in Neudorf, near Ebersdorf. 1749 came to this country with a colony under John Nitschmann. Married Elias Flex and moved to Nazareth.

66. **Anna Maria Schmidt.** iv, n. 7. July 27. Child of the Moravian emigrants, Melchior and Catharine Schmidt.

67. **Christian Schwarz.** ii, s. 7. Dec. 12. An unmarried man. Born 1718, in Brandenburg. His parents were Lutherans. Later he lived in Gnadeck and Herrnhut, uniting with the latter congregation. Went to Silesia as teacher. 1750 came to this country with Brother Jorde's colony of eighty unmarried Brethren. He served as teacher in various places. 1757 received as an acolyte, "Jünger seines Chors."

1767.

68. **Andrew Kremser.** viii, s. 4. Feb. 7. Born in Upper Silesia, Dec. 14, 1711. On the occasion of a visit of Brother Lawatsch and Henry Nitschmann, he was led to Christ. 1739 united with the congregation in Herrnhut. Later lived at Pilgerruh and Herrnhaag. 1743 married Rosina Obersdorf, at the same time with thirty-five other couples. The same year came to this country. Five children survived.

69. **Gottlieb Haberecht.** viii, s. 5. Feb. 28. Widower. Born in Lower Silesia, May 10, 1700. In the great revival in Silesia, 1718-20, he was converted. 1723 married a widow, who was very pious. They often entertained Moravian

exiles. 1732 united with the Herrnhut congregation. 1734 came to Georgia, where his wife died. 1736 to Pennsylvania, where he remained for three years with the Seventh Day Baptists at Ephrata, Lancaster County. 1743 moved to Bethlehem, and later returned to Europe with Count Zinzendorf. 1747 to Algiers, as assistant to Brother Notbeck, the missionary. Ten months later returned to Germany. 1749 to London. 1754 he went to Jamaica, W.I., with Brother Caries, the first missionary to that island. 1759 to Bethlehem and then to Christianspring.

70. **Beatus Schulze.** iii, s. 4. March 2.
71. **Anna Maria Hoepfner.** ix, n. 8. June 24. She had been insane for several years. She was the widow of J. Christopher Hoepfner, who died as missionary on the island of Santa Cruz, 1760.
72. **Jacob Kunz.** iii, s. 5. Nov. 9. An infant.

1768.

73. **David Reichard.** viii, s. 6. Feb. 14. (Gnadenthal) a widower. Born in Hermsdorf, Lower Silesia, March 12, 1713. Led to Christ by Brother Stoehr, who labored among awakened souls in and around Grossburg. 1741 moved to Herrnhut, later to Herrnhaag. After being married, came to this country with a company of colonists. Lived at Fredericktown, Nazareth and Gnadenthal.
74. **Jacob Hafner.** iii, s. 6. May 4. Son of Jacob Hafner. A pupil in Nazareth Hall.

1769.

75. **Anna Barbara Goetje.** vii, n. 1. March 15. Born in Swabia, Feb. 26, 1722. Became acquainted with the Brethren while in Augsburg and was awakened. United with the congregation at Herrnhaag. 1742 came to Pennsylvania, after having married Peter Goetje. Lived in various congregations.
76. **Gottfried Greiter.** ii, s. 8. April 13. An unmarried man, born in Lebanon County, 1740. Parents were Mennonites. His mother, having become acquainted with the Brethren, instructed him in the truths of the gospel and he was led to Christ. Notwithstanding the opposition of friends, he went to Bethlehem in 1754 and later to Christianspring, where he was baptized. He was a very pious young man.
77. **Matthias Bacher.** i, s. 1. May 18. Unmarried man. Born in Salzburg, Feb. 1, 1725. During religious troubles in that country, Lutheran books fell into the hands of his father, with which he and his family and neighbors edified one another, but were, in consequence, persecuted by the Catholic authorities, so that finally he and many others were obliged to leave the country, and came to Ulm, where his parents died soon after. Went to Regensburg, where he became acquainted with members of the Brethren's Church. Went to Ebersdorf, and 1746 was received into the congregation. In 1754 he came, with a company of "single brethren," to Bethlehem. Being sent to Christianspring, he assisted in the building of Nazareth Hall. Later he was "Kinder Bruder" in the school at Bethlehem. 1759 moved to Nazareth Hall, where he appears to have had charge of the boys until 1762. He attended the Provincial Synod at Lititz in 1768. He was a faithful man.

78. **Maria Elizabeth Kunz,** m.n. Minier (Gnadenthal). vii, n. 2. June 25. Born in Conestoga, Pa. Became acquainted with the Brethren in Heidelberg and Bethlehem. Came to Bethlehem when 13 years old. Married David Kunz. Lived at Friedensthal, Nazareth and Gnadenthal. 37 years old.

79. **Wendel Westhoefer.** i, s. 2. Oct. 5. Unmarried man, Christianspring. Born at Muddy Creek, Pa., 1743. Parents members of the Brethren's congregation in Warwick (Lititz). When 16 years old, went to Bethlehem and then to Christianspring. In 1763 received into the congregation.

1770.

80. **David Dietrich Schoenberg.** i, s. 3. July 16. Teacher in Nazareth Hall. Born in Brandenberg, March 23, 1734. A shoemaker by trade. Awakened in his eighteenth year. Visited the Brethren in Neusalz and Gnadenberg, uniting with latter congregation in 1758. Lived in Neusalz until it was destroyed by the Russians, then removed to Gnadenberg with the Brethren, working there in the weavershop. In 1761 was called to Pennsylvania, having been received as an acolyte in Herrnhut, before leaving. He was one of the Brethren engaged in the "hourly intercession." He entered Nazareth Hall as an assistant teacher.

81. **Anna Maria Eyerly.** iv, n. 8. Aug. 9. Infant daughter of Jacob and Christiana Eyerly.

82. **Martin Mordick.** iii, s. 7. Aug. 15. Son of Peter Mordick, a pupil in Nazareth Hall.

83. **David Miller.** iii, s. 8. Aug. 22. Infant son of Henry Miller.

84. **Abraham Hessler.** viii, s. 7. Aug. 23. Born in Thüringia, March 26, 1718. Shoemaker. Awakened in Halle. A soldier, 1741. United with the Brethren in Herrnhaag. Married and then went to Pennsylvania, with many other colonists. Lived in Nazareth, Oley, Bethlehem, Gnadenthal.

85. **George Kaske.** vii, s. 10. Aug. 26. A small child in Nazareth Hall.

86. **John David Kunz.** vii, s. 9. Sept. 24. A child in Nazareth Hall.

1772.

87. **Anna Stotz** (Christianspring). vii, n. 3. Feb. 18. Born in Würtemberg, Jan. 13, 1713. In 1741 married Christian Stotz. In 1750 came to Pennsylvania, with two other married couples.

88. **Gottlieb Berndt.** viii, s. 8. March 16. Born in Hennersdorf, Feb. 19, 1718. Moved to Ebersdorf to learn weaver's trade. Was received into the congregation 1737. In 1749 was called to Pennsylvania, with many others. Married Susannah Ficht.

89. **Susanna Catharine Wohlson,** m.n. Koch. vii, n. 4. Dec. 6. Born in Thüringia, May 15, 1715. Married George Stephen Wohlson, 1734. Awakened by a visiting Brother. 1743 moved to Neudietendorf, and later to Herrnhaag, where she and her husband united with the congregation. 1748 to England, being employed in a school. 1753 to Pennsylvania.

1773.

90. **Jacob Hafner.** ix, s. 9. Feb. 16. Born in Zurich, Switzerland, in 1709. He was a stocking-weaver. Having come to this country, was converted in Philadelphia, through the preaching of Brother Pyrlaeus. United with the Bethlehem

congregation. Married A. Maria Ried. Lived in Nazareth, Gnadenhütten on the Mahony, Gnadenthal, Christianspring.

91. **Margaret Edmonds**, m.n. Anton. vii, n. 5. Feb. 26. Born in New York, March 7, 1721. Awakened by Whitefield's preaching, but led to Christ by the Brethren. 1753 united with the New York congregation. 1755 moved to Bethlehem. Married William Edmonds.

92. **Jacob Pruesing**, (Christianspring.) i, s. 4. April 22. Unmarried. Born on the Island Rügen, July 25, 1709. Came to Herrnhaag in 1745, having been awakened by the Brethren. United with the congregation. 1750 came to this country with a large company of Brethren. Lived in Christianspring.

93. **Anna Elizabeth Gold.** ii, n. 1. July 9. Died of sunstroke while working in the harvest field; 14 years old.

94. **Maria Elizabeth Loesch.** ii, n. 2. Sept. 13. Daughter of John George and Christine Loesch. Born in Tulpehocken, March 11, 1728. 1748 united with Bethlehem congregation. Was appointed Superintendent of the older girls. Later was received as an acolyte.

95. **William Popplewell.** iv, s. 9. Oct. 2. Pupil in Nazareth Hall. Died of small-pox.

1774.

96. **Christian Ernst Walther.** iii, s. 9. April 10. A child, 4 years old.

97. **Maria Christina Hartmann**, m.n. Bauss. vii, n. 6. July 18. Born in the Palatinate, March 28, 1715. 1740 came to this country. 1743 married George Hartmann. One daughter survived (the married sister, Rosina Brunner). United with congregation in Maguntschi. Later moved to Gnadenthal.

98. **Beatus Otto.** vi, s. 9. Nov. 23. Twin son of Joseph and Maria Otto.

99. **Beatus Christ.** vi, s. 10. Dec. 23. Son of Melchior Christ.

1775.

100. **Christian David Ruch.** iv, s. 10. April 13. Infant. Twin.

101. **Anna Maria Ruch.** iii, n. 1. April 29. Infant. Twin.

102. **Beatus Otto.** vi, s. 11. Dec. 15. Infant son of Joseph Otto.

1776.

103. **Magdalene.** ii, n. 3. Aug. 17. Daughter of the negroes Joseph and Hannah, in Christianspring.

1777.

104. **Catharine Blum**, m.n. Steiger. vii, n. 7. Jan. 11. Born in New York, Sept. 1, 1712. 1731 married the widower, Franz Blum. Had eleven children.

105. **John Nicholas Weinland**, (Gnadenthal.) viii, s. 9. Jan. 22. Born Dec. 26, 1706, in Thüringia; 1740, on reading the " Berlin Discourses " of Zinzendorf, he was awakened, and induced by the Brethren to visit Herrnhaag in 1742. The following year moved there and was received into the congregation. In 1749 came to Bethlehem with a large number of colonists. Married Philippine Loesch. He had five children. Together with eleven others, moved to Nazareth in 1754; later to the " Rose Inn," then again to Nazareth and Gnadenthal.

106. **Franz Blum.** ix, s. 10. Jan. 25. Born in the Palatinate, May 1, 1701. Twice married. In 1730 came to Pennsylvania. Converted by Bishop Peter Boehler.

107. **Magdalene Mordick,** (Gnadenthal.) vii, n. 8. March 13. Born July 22, 1717, at Neukirch, Upper Lusatia. While living in the family of Baron von Guldenberg, she became acquainted with Brethren who visited there, and was awakened. Went to Herrnhut in 1742 and was received into the congregation. Later went to Herrnhaag, where she united with a colony, which went to America from Holland and England, with Brother and Sister John Nitschmann. In 1749 married Peter Mordick. Lived for a time at Gnadenhütten on the Mahony. She was a faithful and very pious woman.

108. **John Christian Oerter.** i, s. 5. March 29. An unmarried man. Born in Fredericktown, Oct. 16, 1747, where his parents superintended the school. In the nursery at Nazareth, the Boys' School in Bethlehem and in Nazareth Hall. At Christianspring he learned the gunsmith's trade with Brother Albrecht, and became superintendent of the factory.

109. **Beatus Westhoefer.** iii, s. 10. Nov. 5. His parents lived in Philadelphia. Died while on a visit to Nazareth.

110. **Stephen Bruce.** i, s. 6. Nov. 19. Physician. An unmarried man. Died while here on a visit from Bethlehem. Born in Bethlehem, Nov. 9, 1748. His father was a missionary among the Indians. His widowed mother married Dr. Frederick Otto. He was to learn the locksmith's trade ; but not being very apt, was sent to Dr. Matthew Otto, to study medicine, and succeeded well. A pious young man.

111. **Anna Margaret Loesch,** m.n. Heinsch. vi, n. 1. Dec. 30. Born Dec. 20, 1727, in Bayreuth. In 1745 was received into the congregation. In 1750 came to this country with a large colony, under Brother John Nitschmann. Married twice—to Frederick Beyer, and later to Herman Loesch. From the first marriage a daughter, Anna Rosina, survived ; from the second, three children.

1778.

112. **Matthew Tomerup.** i, s. 7. Feb. 23. Born in Jutland. He was led to Christ by Brother Melchior Zeisberger. United with congregation in Herrnhut, and in 1761 came to this country with Brother and Sister Nathaniel Seidel. Moved to Nazareth, when the Brethren's House in Bethlehem had been converted into a hospital for soldiers. He was a skilful brass and bell founder, and, while at Bethlehem, cast the bell that is now hanging in the steeple of the court-house at Easton.

113. **Beata.** iii, n. 2. June 25. Twin daughter of Jacob and Fredericka Christ.

1779.

114. **David Schmidt.** i, s. 8. Jan. 24. An unmarried man from Christianspring. Born in Bethlehem, Dec. 2, 1758. Son of John and Dorothea Schmidt.

115. **Gottfried Schultze.** viii, s. 10. May 30. Farmer at Nazareth, who died suddenly, when taking his son to Hope, N.J. Born Oct. 10, 1717, in Lower Lusatia. United with the Brethren at Ebersdorf. In 1749 came to America. In Bethlehem married Maria Donewok.

116. **Andrew Holder.** (Christianspring.) ii, s. 9. June 26. Born in New York, April 17, 1731. A linen-weaver. Served in various congregations. Died suddenly.

117. **John Anders.** (Christianspring.) ii, s. 10. Aug. 12. Unmarried. Born in Nazareth, Sept. 23, 1748. When in his seventh year, his parents, with their youngest child, perished at Gnadenhütten on the Mahony, having been killed by the Indians. In 1760 came to Christianspring. On account of bad conduct, excluded for a time from the congregation, but repented and became a very good man.

118. **John Henry Mueller.** ix, s. 11, October 13. Born in Freudenberg, Nassau. Came to this country as a young man and lived at Muddy Creek. Here he became acquainted with visiting brethren and united with the congregation. Married Anna Maria Borall. Aged 55 years.

119. **John Frederick Otto.** viii, s. 11. Dec. 31. Physician. Born Aug. 9, 1712, in Meinungen, Saxony. His father was Dr. John Bernard Otto. He attended universities at Jena and Halle, and graduated at the latter place. His father died in consequence of an accident. Having been awakened through the labors of the Brethren in his native place, he forsook all things and moved to Herrnhaag. The following year he went, via Herrnhut, to Gnadeck in Silesia, where he united with the congregation. In 1743 he married Anna Maria Weber of Frankfort-on-the-Main. During the same year he came, with many colonists, to Bethlehem. He had one son by this union viz., Joseph, (physician at Nazareth, who also had one son) and a daughter, Anna Theodora, who died before her father. His wife died in 1749. In 1750 he married the widow, Mary Magdalene Judith Bruce, m.n. Benezet. In 1760 he was called to Lititz as physician; in 1763 to Nazareth. He was a skillful physician and a very pious man.

1780.

120. **John Biefel.** i, s. 9. March 11. Unmarried. (Christianspring.) Born in Nazareth, Dec. 31, 1746.

121. **Anna Julianne Weckler.** ii, n. 4. June 7. Superintendent of the unmarried sisters. Born May 7, 1718, in Augsburg. In 1744 received into congregation at Herrnhaag; 1748 received as an acolyte; 1752 called to this country. At first had charge of the external affairs of the Bethlehem Sisters' House; 1766 to Nazareth as teacher and superintendent of the single sisters.

122. **John Joseph Lemmert.** i, s. 10. June 20. Unmarried. (Christianspring.) Born in Brisgau, July 15, 1716. A tanner. Received into the Herrnhut congregation 1741. In 1753 came to this country, from London, with a colony. Worked at his trade for eight years, then was employed at Nazareth Hall and at Christianspring. "A childlike, upright, loveable man."

1781.

123. **Jacob Rissler.** i, s. 11. April 4. Unmarried. (Christianspring.) Born in Cassel in Hessen, Sept. 1714. A baker. After having been in a number of cities, went to London, to a sugar refinery. Here became acquainted with Brother Richter, the first missionary to Algiers, and with Zinzendorf. Was received into congregation at Herrnhaag in 1742. With six Brethren went to Livonia. In 1750 came to Bethlehem. Lived in Christianspring.

124. **Anna Marg. Fritsche,** m.n. Vogt. vi, n. 2. April 13. Born Feb. 22, 1723, in Holstein. Awakened by Brethren and Sisters, went to Herrnhaag 1742.

Married, in Marienborn, to Christian Fritsche, in order to go to America. Lived in Nazareth. After death of her husband, married Henry Fritsche.

125. **Joanna Christiana Richter.** ii, n. 5. April 23. Died in Nazareth Hall. Born in Nazareth, March 2, 1756. When two years old, was placed in the nursery. 1780, moved, with other sisters, into the Hall, in order to form a "sisters' choir."

126. **Matthew Spohn.** viii, s. 12. July 16. Christianspring. Born March 1, 1711, in Würtemberg. Married, 1730, Lucia Biezer. In 1750 came to America. Lived in Bethlehem, Nazareth and Christianspring.

127. **Elias Flex,** (Gnadenthal.) ix, s. 12. Sept. 13. Born in Upper Lusatia, Aug. 9, 1713. Received into Herrnhut congregation, May 16, 1742. In 1749 came to America with other colonists, under Brother John Nitschmann. Married Cath. Roney. Blind for a number of years, having lost one eye while cutting wood, and the other while cutting corn.

128. **Joseph.** viii, s. 13. Sept. 29. A negro, born in 1715. When twelve years old he was brought from Guinea to Charleston, S.C., and sold as a slave. Was taken to England in 1727, by the captain of a vessel because he was "a very fine looking negro." In 1732 came to Montserrat, West Indies, and a year later, with ten other slaves, to Durham Furnace, Pennsylvania. His master having moved on a farm about two miles from Bethlehem, Joseph met the Brethren, and from Brother Froehlich heard of Christ the first time, and then desired to be saved. He married a negro woman belonging to the Ysselsteyn family, who lived at Bethlehem; but he was obliged to remain at a furnace in New Jersey. Later was taken to Maryland for two years. His master, having come to Bethlehem and seen Joseph's wife and little son, permitted him to return to the furnace, so that he might be nearer his family. Occasionally he came to Bethlehem, and was impressed by what he there heard. His wife had been baptized. In May, 1752, Joseph was baptized by Bishop Spangenberg in Bethlehem. He longed for liberty and to be able to live in Bethlehem, the Brethren collected £50 and secured his freedom. He lived in Bethlehem for some time; then 12½ years at Gnadenthal, and 10 at Christianspring. Of his seven children, two daughters survived their father.

129. **George Zeisberger.** ix, s. 13. Nov. 26. Born 1688 in Zauchtenthal, Moravia. Baptized by a Catholic priest, but was "brought up" "nach Art und Weise der alten Brüder." Had charge of his father's large estate. Married, 1718, the sister of Brother Töltschig. When the three Nitschmanns, her own brother and her husband's brother, Melchior, left Moravia in 1724, his wife was anxious to follow them. As only bonds and afflictions awaited them, and Zeisberger had been cited to appear before government officials, they left, "empty handed," with their three little children, coming to Herrnhut in 1726. He became superintendent of the estate at Berthelsdorf, where his wife died. Married, in Herrnhut, Anna Böhm, from Kune-walde, in Moravia. In 1743 he was called to Bethlehem with many others. Later he moved to Gnadenthal, and superintended the clearing of the land and establishing of the farms. Died at Gnadenthal, aged 93 years. His wife had died in 1758.

1782.

130. **Joanna Elizabeth Kern.** iii, n. 3. May 3. An infant.

131. **John Lischer.** viii, s. 14. May 12. Born Nov. 28, 1719, in Witgenstein. His parents were Mennonites. After his father's death, he and his mother came to America, and in 1742 became acquainted with the Brethren, who led him to the Saviour; 1743 was baptized in Oley by Andrew Eschenbach and soon after came to Bethlehem. In 1746, he was received as an acolyte; 1753 he went, with a number of unmarried brethren, to Wachovia, N. C., and assisted in the founding of the first congregations. Returning, after his second visit to North Carolina and several years' residence there, he married Maria Catharine Loesch, in Bethlehem, 1759. He had four children. He had charge of the Crown Inn, on the south side of the Lehigh; later, of the Rose Inn, and finally of the Inn at Nazareth until 1775. During the last years of his life, he had charge of the graveyard.

132. **Daniel Kamm.** ii, s. 11. July 1. Unmarried; (Christianspring). Born in Würtemberg, Jan. 19, 1715. A shoemaker by trade. In 1734 he traveled and came to Frankfort on the Main, where he became acquainted with the Brethren. Later to Marienborn, where he was received into the congregation. In 1741 to Herrnhaag. In 1746 received a call as missionary to Berbice, British Guiana, being received as an acolyte before leaving Zeist. In 1747 he went with Niels Clarup to Berbice, serving in Pilgerruh nine years. In 1756 he came to Bethlehem, being in feeble health. In 1759 received a call to Surinam and went there with Brother and Sister Meiser, serving at Sharon. In consequence of an attack by hostile blacks, in 1761, he was obliged to flee. He came to Bethlehem via New England. Became sick nurse in the Brethren's House in Bethlehem and later in Christianspring. He was a very faithful man and greatly beloved.

133. **John Weiss.** iii, s. 11. July 9. Child of "Commissioner" Weiss, of Easton. Brought by mother and grandmother to be buried here.

134. **Samuel Flex.** i, s. 12. Oct. 1. Unmarried man. (Christianspring.) Born in Nazareth, Jan. 30, 1751. Together with fourteen unmarried brethren, he moved into the new Brethren's House in Nazareth in 1774, May 18.

135. **Jacob Loesch.** ix, s. 14. Nov. 8. Born Nov. 22, 1722, near Schoharie, N.Y. His parents were George and Anna Loesch, of Gnadenthal. When Christianspring was begun in 1749, he went there as warden of the Brethren's House; 1753 appointed warden of the colony of unmarried brethren, who went to North Carolina, accompanied by Bishop Nathaniel Seidel and Gottlob Königsdörfer. In 1757 married Anna Blum in Bethlehem. He had five children. 1758 went again to North Carolina, and was made Justice of the Peace of Rowan County. The affairs in Bethabara occasioned much labor and trouble. Remained seven years in Bethabara. In 1771 removed to Nazareth as Superintendent of the property of the "Administration," and also Justice of the Peace. On his way to Hope, N.J., he fell from his horse and died in a house 11 miles from Nazareth.

136. **Philip Jacob Meyer.** i, s. 13. Nov. 29. Born in 1722 in Würtemberg. While traveling as a journeyman shoemaker, enlisted as a soldier while intoxicated. Later he deserted, and in his wanderings came to Calmar, Upper Lusatia, where he was awakened, through the efforts of the Brethren.

Thence he went to Basle and Herrnhaag, uniting with the latter congregation. In 1750 came to this country with twenty-nine unmarried brethren. Lived in Bethlehem, Christianspring and Nazareth. " Ein gutes, seliges Herz." Loved and honored.

137. **John George Schnell.** viii, s. 15. Dec. 15. Born Jan. 4, 1713, in Eyb, Frankenland. On his travels, was awakened at Nuremberg. Hearing of Herrnhut, he came there in 1739, and was received into the congregation the following year; 1741 married at Marienborn, Helena Hensch. In 1766 received a call to Jamaica, and was ordained a Deacon. He was stationed at Carmel; 1771 was called to Bethlehem and later to Nazareth, where he carried on his business as a linen-weaver.

138. **A. Christina Loesch,** m.n. Wallborn. ix, n. 9. Dec. 17. Wife of John George Loesch. Born July 24, 1700, in Wisbad, Nassau, not far from the Rhine. In her tenth year, came with her parents to New York; later moved to Schoharie, where she was married. Had eleven children. In 1723 moved to Tulpehocken, where they did not hear God's Word till 1735, when the awakened preacher of Skippach, Leybecker, came there and led the family to the Saviour. Later became acquainted with Spangenberg and the Brethren, who sent Brother Büttner and later Philip Meurer as ministers to them. In 1745 was received into the Brethren's Church, at the Synod at Quittopahilla, near Lebanon. They became members of the Heidelberg congregation until the congregation at Quittopahilla was organized. Later moved to Gnadenthal.

139. **Henry Fritsche.** viii, s. 16. Dec. 24. Born Jan. 8, 1715, in Lower Silesia. On his travels became acquainted with the Brethren and was awakened. Came to Herrnhut in 1742, and was received into the congregation. In 1748 came to America with a colony under Brother John Nitschmann. In 1749 married Catharine Helena Wentzel, from Silesia. Moved to Nazareth. After the death of his wife, married the widow of Christian Fritsche, Anna Margaretha, m.n. Vogt.

1783.

140. **Joanna Schaefer.** vi, n. 3. March 24. A daughter of I. M. Ysselsteyn. Died suddenly, while feeding her sheep in the barn. Born April 16, 1728, near Albany, N. Y. Having moved to Pennsylvania, living on the south side of the Lehigh, near Bethlehem, Zinzendorf visited them and held services in their house. After her father's death, she and her mother moved to Bethlehem, where they united with the congregation. In 1746 married Nicholas Schaefer. As midwife she assisted at the birth of 130 children.

141. **Peter Mordick.** ix, s. 15. May 6. Widower, Gnadenthal; found dead in bed. Born Feb. 17, 1716, in Holstein. 1748 received into congregation at Herrnhaag. Both in Romburg and Marienborn he was the coachman for the Countess Zinzendorf. In 1749 came to Bethlehem. Married Magdalene Schwarz, of Neukirch, Upper Lusatia. He lived in various congregations.

142. **John David Kern.** iii, s. 12, July 23. An infant.

143. **Azarias Smith.** ix, s. 16. Sept. 23. Died in consequence of a fall from a horse. Born Dec. 17, 1742, in Lebanon, Conn. Parents converted by Whitefield. Later became acquainted with the Brethren, and having been

awakened, moved to Bethlehem, then to Christianspring, where he was received into the congregation. In 1763 "Hausdiener" in Nazareth Hall; 1782 married Joanna Eliz. Ashley.

1784.

144. **John George Krieckbaum.** i, s. 14. Jan. 14. Born Feb. 12, 1713, in Brandenburg. At Nuremberg was awakened by the Brethren. United with Herrnhaag congregation in 1743. In 1751 came to Pennsylvania. Served in various capacities in Bethlehem and Nazareth; finally as cook in the Brethren's House.

145. **Beatus Smith.** iv, s. 11. March 6. Son of Azarias Smith.

146. **Beata Jag.** iii, n. 4. March 23.

147. **Molly Edmonds.** ii, n. 6. June 24. Born on Long Island, Oct. 11, 1744. Lived in Nazareth Hall, with other sisters.

1785.

148. **Matthew Hanke.** ix, s. 17. Jan. 2. Born Jan. 17, 1707, in Upper Silesia. When 13 years of age, he was hired to a farmer, who was a Christian. He was awakened, came to Herrnhut and was received into the congregation. In 1743 married and came to Bethlehem; 1744 to Nazareth. Was twice married.

149. **Anna Rosina Brunner.** iii, n. 5. Feb. 25. An infant.

150 **Christian Schmidt.** i, s. 15. April 12. Unmarried. Born in Jutland, Oct. 17, 1696; awakened by the preaching of a student in Holstein. In 1746 went to Herrnhaag; 1748 to Bethlehem; 1754 Christianspring.

151. **John Schuerzer.** ii, s. 12. July 1. Born in the Palatinate, July 24, 1743. In his 13th year was baptized by the Mennonites, to whom his parents belonged. In 1763 to Marienborn and was received into the congregation; 1770 to America.

152. **Franz Christian Lembke.** xi, s. 1. July 11. For almost 30 years pastor of the Nazareth congregation. Born July 13, 1704, in Baden, his father being an Evangelical Lutheran minister, his mother a Jewess. He studied in the Gymnasium in Durbach and the Strassburg University, becoming "Magister" there in 1725. He also attended various universities, amongst these Erfurt and Leipsic. In 1735 was called to Strasburg as preceptor in the Gymnasium and "Sunday Evening Preacher" in old St. Peter's Church. In 1736 married Anna Salome Schwerdt, who died in 1743. Of his two children, a son survived. On account of his intimacy with the Brethren and especially Zinzendorf, he was forbidden to preach. The same year, 1745, he united with the Brethren's Church. Receiving his dismissal from the Strasburg Gymnasium, he went to Herrnhaag in 1746, with his son. In 1748 was received as an acolyte; 1749 was ordained a Deacon of the Church, in London; 1750-53 served as preacher of the "Exiles' Church" in Herrnhaag; 1754 was called to America. Married Margaret Catharine Wyk of London; 1755 ordained as presbyter; 1755-56 pastor of the Warwick (Lititz) congregation; Jan. 20, 1757, minister at Nazareth (having apparently previously served here a short time before going to Lititz); 1763, also Director or Principal of Nazareth Hall, and in 1770 a member of the Provincial Helpers' Conference, continuing as pastor. At the close of 1784 he resigned as pastor, on account

of failing health, and the following year moved to Old Nazareth from Nazareth Hall, serving, however, as " Haus Liturgus" or chaplain in Old Nazareth. He was a very able, faithful and beloved man.

153. **Lorenz Nilson.** ii, s. 13. July 21. Born Dec. 8, 1715, in Holstein. In 1749 was received into congregation in Zeist; 1754 to Bethlehem, living in various congregations. A faithful, earnest man of God.

154. **John Dealing.** ix, s. 18. Sept. 10. Born in West Jersey, May 17, 1746. His pious parents brought him to Bethlehem to study medicine with Dr. Matthew Otto; 1762 was received into the congregation. In 1769 went to Wachovia to Brother Jacob Bonn, the physician; 1769 married Maria Magdalene Graff, in Lancaster, and moved to Philadelphia, to practice his profession. In 1776 to Bethlehem; 1781 to Old Nazareth and later to Nazareth.

155. **Rosina Bernhard,** m. n. Gall. vi, n. 4. Sept. 12. Born in Silesia, March 25, 1709. In 1739 went to Herrnhut; 1749 came to Bethlehem. Married Wenzel Bernhard and lived in various congregations.

156. **George Stephen Wohlson.** viii, s. 17. Oct. 17. Born Aug. 19, 1707, near Erfurt. 1746 to Herrnhaag with his family; 1753 to America. A very good man, " living very near to the Lord."

157. **Susanna Mary Ari.** ii, n. 7. Dec. 17. A mulatto. Born in Christianspring. Aged 13 years.

1786.

158. **Samuel Lauck.** i, s. 16. Jan. 12. Born Jan. 30, 1713, at Rüdenhausen. At the suggestion of Rev. J. Paul Weiss, came to Herrnhut. Went to Halle for three years, laboring amongst the awakened soldiers there ; 1744, received into the congregation at Herrnhaag; 1750 to Bethlehem. Served in various capacities in Christianspring and later in the school at Maguntschi (Emmaus). He led an exemplary life.

159. **Beata Brucker.** iii, n. 6. Feb. 12. An infant.

160. **John Schmidt.** viii, s. 18. Feb. 17. (Christianspring.) Born April 1, 1708, in Upper Silesia, parents Catholics. His father was killed in battle with the Turks. His pious mother instructed him in the truths of evangelical religion; 1737 went to Herrnhut; later to Pilgerruh and Herrnhaag, and superintended the erection of the first Brethren's House; 1749 to America. Married Dorothea Vogt. Lived in various congregations. Finally was cook in Nazareth Hall.

161. **Anna Maria Michler,** widow Schropp, m. n. Thome. vi, n. 5. April 3. Born in Basle. Visited in Herrnhaag and was so impressed that she resolved never to return to her home; was received into the congregation. In 1743 married Matthew Schropp and came to Bethlehem, serving with him in Nazareth and Wachovia. Her husband died in Wachovia in 1766, and she returned to Bethlehem, moving into the Widows' House. In 1778 she married the Rev. Wolfang Michler, and with him served in Schoeneck and and later in Hebron. Her husband having died, she moved to Nazareth. By her first marriage, she had six children of whom two sons and two daughters survived their mother. Aged 67.

162. **Frederick Ziegler.** xi, s. 2. May 17. Born near Stuttgart, Nov. 30, 1721. In 1741 came to this country. Was awakened in a meeting held by Brother

Christian Henry Rauch, in Lancaster; 1747 received into the Bethlehem congregation; 1759 married Anna Cath. Koch.

163. **Michael Muecke.** xi, s. 3. May 30. Born 1708, in Hillersdorf, Upper Silesia. His father was a Catholic, his mother Lutheran. When fourteen years old, united with the Lutheran Church; but, being in great spiritual unrest, he came to Herrnhut, then to Pilgerruh, then to Herrnhaag, where he united with the congregation in 1741. In 1743 was received as an acolyte, and, at the same time with twenty-four others, was married, and went to Pennsylvania. Lived in various congregations. " He lived in intimate union with the Saviour." His wife died in 1755; he had four sons.

164. **Anna Julianna Christ**, m.n. Herbach. ix, n. 10. June 22. Born in York, Pa., Aug. 28, 1752. In her seventeenth year came to Lititz and united with the congregation. In 1755 married Peter Christ; 1785 moved to Nazareth; she had five children.

165. **Daniel Oesterlein.** xi, s. 4. Aug. 13. Born in Ulm, April 6, 1712. In 1739 came to this country. He was married in 1746 to Susanna E. Werner, who died at Bethlehem, in 1803. Lived in various congregations.

166. **William Edmonds.** xi, s. 5. Sept. 15. Widower. Born in Colford, Gloucestershire, England, Oct. 24, 1708. A member of the Episcopal Church. In 1736 came to America. 1739 married Rebecca DeBeavoises. He had four children. In 1741 became acquainted with the Brethren, and became concerned about his salvation. After the death of his wife in 1747, he served as cook on the ship *Irene*, on her voyage to Holland and England. In 1749 came to Bethlehem. He worked in the tannery, at the ferry and in the store. In 1755 he married Margaret Anthony, of New York. In Oct. of that year, he was elected a member of the Assembly, in Pennsylvania, for Northampton County. In 1763 opened a store near Nazareth; survived by one son and two daughters.

167. **Johanna Rosina Mueksch**, m.n. Kuhn. vi, n. 6. Dec. 25. Born Nov. 15, 1717, in Goerlitz, Upper Lusatia. Received her first religious impressions in the orphan-school in Sorau. In 1735 moved to Herrnhut and was received into the congregation. In 1739 to Lindheim, in the service of the wife of Von Schrautenbach. In 1741, in Marienborn, married Michael Muecksch, and left for Pennsylvania via Holland and England. In 1742 a son was born, on the voyage, dying soon after. Lived in various congregations. She had eight children, of whom four sons and two daughters survived. Her eldest son was Nathaniel.

1787.

168. **Anna Maria Haller**, m.n. Hundsecker. vi, n. 7. June 6. Born Sept. 2, 1719, in Breitfurt. In 1738 came to Pennsylvania; 1740 married Henry Haller; 1743 was awakened by the preaching of Jacob Lischy; 1746 she and her husband united with congregation at Muddy Creek, and they served the congregation there, at Fredericktown and Allemängel. In 1755-79 lived in Lititz; 1779 in Gnadenthal, where her husband was warden. An excellent midwife and assisted at the birth of 500 children.

169. **Anna Dorothea Weinert**, m.n. Unger. vi, n. 8. Dec. 7. Born 1720 in Schwabach; 1743 received into congregation at Herrnhaag. In 1743

married Christian Weinert. In company with 120 persons, came to Pennsylvania, living in Nazareth.

1788.

170. **Christian David Brucker.** iii, s. 13. Jan. 9. A child.

171. **Magdalene Brucker,** m.n. Stotz. viii, n. 9. Feb. 7. Born in Würtemberg, Nov. 21, 1744. In 1750 came to America, with her parents; 1757 received into Nazareth congregation; later lived at Lititz. In 1781 married Christian Demuth and moved to Hope, N.J., where her husband died the same year. In 1782 she married David Brucker.

172. **Matthew Muecke.** iv, s. 12. March 12. A child.

173. **John Henry Haller.** xi, s. 6. April 10. Widower. Born in Alsace, Sept. 2, 1719. In 1733, came with his parents to America. In 1740 married Anna Maria Hundsecker, with whom he lived nearly 47 years. Awakened by the preaching of Jacob Lischy, they pledged themselves to live, not to themselves, but to Christ alone. He served as minister at Muddy Creek, Fredericktown and Allemängel. In 1755 he superintended the farms at Lititz; 1779-85, warden in Gnadenthal.

174. **Anna Johanna Seidel,** m.n. Piesch. xi, n. 1. April 11. Born in Berthelsdorf, Jan. 12, 1726, where her parents, who had come from Moravia the previous autumn, were living temporarily. After the death of her mother, when she was six years old, she entered the orphans' house in Herrnhut. In 1738, together with other children, she went to Berlin and thence to Marienborn, where she was received into the congregation, and later became an acolyte. In 1740 moved, with the scholars of the girls' school, to Herrnhaag. In 1741 became superintendent of the children. In 1745 became "laboress of the single sisters" in Herrnhaag and in 1747 general laboress or elder of all the classes of unmarried sisters. During the following years she was principally in the "Jüngerhaus," and in 1752 went on a visit to America. On Oct. 30, 1760, married Brother Nathaniel Seidel and went to America. She faithfully assisted her husband in his duties, and with him, a member of the Provincial Board, visited the congregations. She also attended the Synod at Marienborn in 1769, with her husband. After his death, May 17th, 1782, she left Bethlehem, where she had resided during more than twenty years, removing to Nazareth, where she served as the "laboress" or spiritual superintendent of the Widows. "She had received from the Lord extraordinary gifts, being both possessed of superior intellectual power and also of executive ability. The attention of Count Zinzendorf was drawn to her already in her childhood, and, at an early age, important duties were entrusted to her. Her services, both in European congregations and in those in this country, were appreciated, and she was held in loving remembrance and highly esteemed."

175. **Mary.** vii, n. 9. Aug. 8. A negro, the wife of Peter. Born in Guinea, in 1736, belonging to the Mandango nation. In 1762 she was seized by a ship captain, taken to America and sold. In 1763 married Peter. In 1775 was employed in the family of Brother Henry Van Vleck, Sr. She was led to Christ, and in 1780 was baptized in Bethlehem. Bro. Van Vleck having effected the freedom of her and her husband, they moved to Old Nazareth in 1784. At first she longed to return to Guinea, where she had been the

daughter of the chief of the Mandango nation and was well cared for ; but later she recognized the wonderful leading of the Lord, with gratitude.

176. **Catharine Ernst.** ii, n. 8. Aug. 29. A girl in Old Nazareth. Born in Bethlehem, April 9, 1771. In 1779 to Emmaus, with her parents; 1783 returned to Nazareth.

177. **Beatus Krause.** iv, s. 13. Oct. 30. Infant of Matthew and Anna B. Krause.

178. **Anna Christ**, m.n. Wolfer. ix, n. 11. Dec. 4. Born in Lauffen, Würtemberg, Oct. 1, 1711. In 1733 married Rudolph Christ. 1750, came with her six children to Pennsylvania, living in Bethlehem, uniting with that congregation. They resided in Friedensthal, Bethlehem and Gnadenthal. After the death of her husband, she lived, for some time, in the Bethlehem Widows' House, and since 1772 at Nazareth, with her son Jacob. " Her joy was in the Lord, by whose blood she had been redeemed."

179. **Anna Maria Boehmer**, m.n. Essig. viii, n. 10. Dec. 4. Born in Swabia, Aug. 24, 1718. Her parents having died while she was very young, she went to Herrnhaag, having been awakened by the Brethren, and was received into the congregation. Married Martin Boehmer, with whom and twenty-three newly married couples, she went to Pennsylvania.

180. **Justina Julianna Bader**, m.n. Seidel. ix, n. 12. Dec. 8. Born in Breithard, Nassau-Usingen, July 1728, where her father was a minister. After his death, in her thirteenth year, she came to Ebersdorf, where she united with the congregation. In 1749 to Herrnhaag and thence, with others, to Pennsylvania. In 1754 married Brother Philip Christoph Bader, and with him served in many congregations.

1789.

181. **Elizabeth Kemble**, m.n. Chaplain. vi, n. 9. Jan. 12. A widow. Born in Philadelphia, Dec. 18, 1725. Her parents were Thomas and Anna Chaplain. Her father was a pilot. Married Thomas Archdall, in Philadelphia, April 12, 1750. He died twenty months later. Two years later, married Francis Robinson, who died in 1757. In 1763 married George Kemble, a widower, with six children. He died in 1774. By her second marriage she had two children ; a daughter survived her, Elizabeth, who married Jacob Weiss.

182. **Anna Rosina Belling**, m.n. Kremser. viii, n. 11. June 27. Born in Nazareth, Sept. 22, 1745. Her father was Andrew Kremser. Married Gottfried Belling in Nazareth, Dec. 3, 1782. Two sons, Henry Gottfried and John Andrew, survived.

183. **Christian Louis Schnepf.** iii, s. 14. Aug. 4. A child of upwards of four years, an inmate of the school. His parents were Louis and Hannah Schnepf, missionaries in St. Thomas, W. I., where he was born.

184. **Anna Maria Giersch.** iii, n. 7. Sept. 5. Infant daughter of Christian and Elizabeth Giersch.

185. **Anna Joanna Levering.** iii, n. 8. Dec. 28. Infant daughter of Joseph and Elizabeth (Ashley) Levering.

1790.

186. **Andrew Brocksch.** i, s, 17. Jan. 6. Unmarried. (Christianspring.) Born Oct. 8, 1702, in Bürgerwald, Upper Silesia.

187. **Michael Ruch.** ii, s. 14. Jan. 7. Unmarried. (Christianspring.) Born Sept. 29, 1718, in Würtemberg.

188. **Johanna Rosina Schaefer.** iii, n. 9. Jan. 17. Infant daughter of Fred. and Anna Rosina Schaefer.

189. **Beatus Brucker.** iii, s. 15. Feb. 11. Infant son of John David and Elizabeth (Schneider) Brucker.

190. **Carl Erdman Oehme.** iv, s. 14. May 6. Infant son of John Erdman Gotthelf and Elizabeth Oehme.

191. **John David Brucker.** xi, s. 7. June 30. Born in Bethlehem, Sept. 3, 1742. His father, John Brucker, died as missionary in St. Jan, W. I., in 1764. In 1781 married the widow, Magdalene Demuth, m.n. Stotz. In 1789 married Elizabeth Schneider.

192. **John Christian Micksch.** iv, s. 15. Aug. 7. Infant son of Christian and Anna P. Micksch.

193. **George Loesch.** xi, s. 8. Aug. 15. Born April 23, 1699, in Gernsheim, near Worms. His parents were Balthazar and Susanna P. Loesch. In 1721 married Christine Wallborn in New York, with whom he lived sixty-one years. He united with the Brethren while living at Tulpehocken, Pa. He had eleven children, fifty grandchildren and fifty great grandchildren.

194. **Johanna Elizabeth Levering.** vii, n. 10. Oct. 17. Born April 11, 1753, in Rochester, N.Y. In 1782 married Azarias Smith, in Nazareth, who was killed by a fall from a horse. July 27, 1787, married Joseph Levering.

195. **Abraham Levering.** iii, s. 16. Oct. 26. Infant son of Joseph and Johanna Levering

196. **Susanna Philippina Weinland,** m.n. Loesch. vi, n. 10. Nov. 28. A widow. Born in Tulpehocken, Pa., June 23, 1723. Daughter of George and Christine Loesch. Aug., 1749, married John Nicholas Weinland, in Bethlehem, who died in 1777.

1791.

197. **Beatus Kern.** iv, s. 16. Jan. 21. Infant twin-son of John Michael Kern.

198. **Frederick David Kern.** iv, s. 17. Feb. 8. Infant twin-son of J. M. Kern.

199. **Johanna Rosina Miksch.** iv, n. 9. Mar. 10. Child of Nathaniel and Anna M. Miksch.

200. **George Christoph Hepner.** ii, s. 15. Mar. 22. Unmarried. Christiansspring. Born in Linda, Saxony. Aged 78.

201. **John Frederick Boehner.** ii, s. 16. April 10. Unmarried. (Christiansspring.) Born May 18, 1845, in St. Thomas, W. I., where his parents, John and Veronica (Loehans) Boehner, were missionaries.

202. **Renatus Theodore Reichel.** iv, s. 18. April 29. Infant son of Brother and Sister Carl Gotthold and Anna Dorothea (Maas) Reichel, minister at Nazareth.

203. **Susanna Catharine Hartmann,** m.n Ficht. vii, n. 11. Aug. 5. (Gnadenthal.) Born May 6, 1726, in Neundorf, near Ebersdorf. In 1749 married Gottlieb Berndt, who died in 1772. Married George Hartmann, 1775.

204. **John Scheffler.** i, s. 18. Aug. 18. Unmarried. (Christianspring.) Born Dec. 28, 1715, in Niederbrunn, Alsace.

3

205. **Christian Stotz.** xi, s. 9. Aug. 20. Widower. (Christianspring.) Born in Lauffen, Würtemberg, May 19, 1711. Married Anna Herr, who died in 1769. Surviving children : Lewis, in Lancaster, Pa.; Samuel, in Salem, N. C.; Anna Maria, in Salem, N. C.

1792.

206. **Sybilla Elizabeth Belling.** iv, n. 10. Jan. 30. Child of Gottfried and Mary (Edmonds) Belling. Died of small-pox.
207. **Anna Theodora Schaefer.** iii, n. 10. Feb. 3. Child. Died of small-pox.
208. **August Schloesser.** xi, s. 10. May 3. Born Aug. 3, 1727, in Rodenwals, Moravia. In 1773 married Mary Edmonds.
209. **Wenzel Bernhard.** xi, s. 11. May 26. (Christianspring.) Born Sept. 28, 1716, in Schärma, Bohemia. 1749 married Rosina Gall, in Bethlehem.
210. **Michael Miksch.** xi, s. 12. June 28. (Gnadenthal). Born in Kunewalde, Moravia, Sept. 27, 1710. In 1741, married Johanna Rosina Kuhn in Herrnhaag, who died Dec. 25, 1786, after a married life of 45 years. Eight children, of whom six survived the father; viz.: Nathaniel, born Sept. 21, 1743 ; David Miksch (Christianspring); Anna Rosina (living in Nazareth); Dorothea, married to Massah Warner, of Bethlehem : John Christian, married to Anna P. Loesch ; Paul Miksch, Brethren's laborer and assistant warden in Christianspring.
211. **George Gold.** xi, s. 13. Aug. 29. Born April 23, 1722, in Zauchtenthal, Moravia. Married Anna Maria Roth, in Bethlehem.
212. **Anna Maria Kremser,** m.n. Beischer. vi, n. 11. Sept. 3. Born Oct. 4, 1763, in Sussex County, New Jersey. Married March 14, 1790, John Kremser, who was inn-keeper at Nazareth. One son survived.

1793.

213. **John Frederick Peissert.** vii, s. 11. Feb. 16. Infant child of Christoph and Rosina (Frevel) Peissert.
214. **Christian Belling.** vi, s. 12. Feb. 21. Child of Gottfried Belling.
215. **Frederick Danke.** xi, s. 14. April 18. Born near Hannover, Aug. 19, 1745. Married Anna Maria Clewell, 1779. Four children survived : viz., John Frederick, John, Franz Christian, and Maria Magdalena.
216. **Beatus Proske.** vi, s. 13. Aug. 2. Infant son of George and Maria Proske.
217. **David Miksch.** ii, s. 17. Aug. 27. Son of Michael Miksch. Unmarried. (Christianspring.) Born Nov. 27, 1745, in Bethlehem.
218. **Christian Ludwig Grunewald.** ii, s. 18. Nov. 9. Unmarried. (Christianspring.) Born in Priegnitz, Brandenburg, Sept. 29, 1721.

1794.

219. **Anna Maria Schenk,** m.n. Kling. viii, n. 12. June 24. Born in Lancaster Co., Pa., Jan. 23, 1739. Married Sept., 1778, in Bethlehem, to Martin Schenk.
220. **Justina Eleonora Bader.** ii, n. 9. Nov. 22. Unmarried. Born in Lancaster, Pa., April 4, 1759. Her parents were Philip Christian and Justina Julianna (Seidel) Bader, her father a minister of the Church.

1795.

221. **Margaretha Schloesser**, m.n. Edmonds. vii, n. 12. Feb. 13. Born in New York, May 4, 1739. Her parents were William and Margaretha (Beavoises) Edmonds. Married August Schloesser in 1737, who died in 1792.

222. **Christian Foerster.** xiii, s. 1. May 19. Unmarried. Born Oct. 1, 1736, in Geibsdorf, Upper Lusatia.

223. **Franz Seiffert.** xiii, s. 2. July 1. Unmarried. Born Dec. 16, 1728, in Grulich, Bohemia.

224. **George Kaske.** xi, s. 15. July 6. Born March 2, 1712, in Gottschdorf, Upper Lusatia. Married, 1746, Elizabeth Funk. Four children survived. Renatus, born in Berbice, married Anna Eva Heyn, in Nazareth; Elizabeth, married to John Stotz of Bethlehem; Joseph, in Nazareth.

225. **John Christoph Weinert.** xi, s. 16. July 19. Born in Upper Lusatia, March 15, 1712. Married to Anna Dorothea Unger.

226. **Beatus Peissert.** vii, s. 12.

227. **Johann Nicolaus Funk.** xiii, s. 3. Aug. 12. Unmarried. Born Nov. 10, 1720, at Neudorf, Voigtland. Aged 74 years.

228. **David Miksch.** vii, s. 13. Aug. 18. Infant son of Nathaniel and Anna Maria (Fritsch) Miksch.

229. **Christian Lewis Miksch.** vii, s. 14. Aug. 24. Infant son of John Christian and Philippine (Loesch) Miksch.

230. **Henry Daniel Schmick.** vii, s. 15. Sept. 17. Infant son of Jacob and Anna Johanna (Krause) Schmick.

231. **Jacob Schmick.** vii, s. 16. Oct. 2. Infant son of Jacob Schmick.

1796.

232. **Martin Boehmer.** xi, s. 17. March 22. Born March 9, 1717, near Löbau. 1743 married Anna M. Essig, who died Dec. 4, 1788.

233. **John Jacob Eyerly.** xii, s. 1. March 31. Stricken with apoplexy while in the field. Born July 17, 1716, at Dürmenz, in Würtemberg. Married Aug. 25, 1755, Christina Schwarz. One son and two daughters survived, viz: John Jacob, married Anna Maria Frey; Maria Elizabeth, married Owen Rice; Anna Christina, married Christian Henry Beck.

234. **Maria Magdalene Bollinger.** vi, n. 12. April 24. (Gnadenthal.) Born in Lancaster Co., Pa. Parents, Peter and Magdalene Bollinger. Married Henry Bollinger.

235. **Michael Moehring.** xii, s. 2. April 30. Born Sept. 6, 1739, in Hirschberg, Voigtland. Married, 1775, to Elizabeth Rauschenberger.

236. **Elizabeth Bollinger.** iv, n. 11. May 5. Infant daughter of Henry Bollinger.

237. **Nathaniel Louis Reichel.** iii, s. 18. June 24. Son of Carl Gotthold Reichel, pastor. (Small-pox.)

238. **Christian Matthiesen.** xiii, s. 4. June 29. Unmarried. (Christianspring.) Born in Jutland, Feb. 2, 1712.

239. **Elizabeth Horsfield.** iii, n. 11. Aug. 13. Infant daughter of William and Rebecca (Weiss) Horsfield, storekeeper at Nazareth.

240. **Susanna Miksch.** iv, n. 12. Aug. 13. Infant daughter of John Christian and Anna P. Miksch.

241. **Judith Edmonds.** ii, n. 10. Sept. 14. Unmarried. Born in Bethlehem, Oct. 14, 1756. Parents, William and Margaret (Anton) Edmonds.

242. **Philip Jacob Hoeger.** xiii, s. 5. Nov. 4. Unmarried. (Christianspring.)
Born in Friesach, Germany, May 1, 1728.

1797.

243. **Jane Henry.** iii, n. 12. Jan. 22. Infant daughter of William and Sabina
(Schropp) Henry.

244. **Ludwig Biefel.** xiii, s. 6. March 13. Unmarried. (Christianspring.) Born
in Nazareth, July 28, 1752.

245. **Philip Christian Bader.** xii, s. 3. March 15. Born July 15, 1715, in Hangen-
bietenheim, near Strasburg, Lower Alsatia, where his father was minister.
Parents were John Nicholas and Anna Barbara (Cunow) Bader. In his twenty-
fifth year ordained as minister. In 1747 he united with the Brethren's Church,
and served several years in the Paedagogium in Schlössel, near Gnadenfrei, and
in Gross Hennersdorf, near Herrnhut. In 1751 came to Pennsylvania, and
served in various congregations as pastor, and especially in Lancaster and
Hebron (near Lebanon). May 16, 1762, ordained as Presbyter. In 1754,
Jan. 10, married Justina Julianna Seidel, who died Dec. 8, 1788.

246. **Michael Ruch.** xii, s. 4. May 9. Born Jan. 20, 1727, in Eckendorf, Alsace.
Married the widow, Maria Christina Walther, m.n. Beck, in 1771. Died
of cancer in the hand.

247. **Christian Giersch.** xii, s. 5. June 5. Born June 23, 1724, in Schoenau, in
Moravia. Married, June, 1772, Elizabeth Gerhard. Four children survived:
Elizabeth, Rosina, Christian Frederick and Joseph.

248. **Joseph Levering.** xii, s. 6. June 6. Born in Nazareth, March 28, 1755.
His parents were John and Susannah (Bechtel) (Merk) Levering. His father
died in Jamaica and his mother in St. Jan, W. I. Married, July 27, 1787,
Johanna Elizabeth Smith, m.n. Ashley, who died in Nazareth, Oct. 17, 1790.
Both of the children by this marriage died. On June 5, 1791, married Anna
Catharine Clewell. Three children survived: Anna Rosina, Catharine
Louisa and Charles Joseph. The latter was born Jan. 23, 1795.

249. **Catharine Margaret Schmidt,** m.n. Fischer. xi, n. 2. Aug. 17. Born April
18, 1726, in Ebersdorf. July 15, 1749, married Melchior Schmidt in Bethlehem. Her eldest daughter, Julianna, was married to John Beitel, of Nazareth.

250. **Anna Maria Gold.** ii, n. 11. Aug. 18. Unmarried. Born in Gnadenthal,
July 15, 1753.

251. **Renatus Belling.** vi, s. 14. Sept. 9. Infant son of Gottfried and Maria
(Edmonds) Belling.

252. **Frederick Nathaniel Weber.** xiii, s. 7. Sept. 11. Unmarried. (Christianspring.) Born in Bethlehem, May 18, 1766.

253. **Beatus Miksch.** vi, s. 15. Oct. 10. Infant son of Paul and Catharine
(Busch) Miksch.

254. **John Martin Schenk.** xii, s. 7. Dec. 6. Deacon of the Church. Born
Nov. 12, 1733, in Zauchtenthal, Moravia. Married, Sept. 2, 1778, Anna
Maria Kling, in Bethlehem, who died in 1794, in Nazareth. In 1795 married
Anna Marg. Mueller, m.n. Schwalb.

255. **John David Kunz.** xii, s. 8. Dec. 9. Born in Zauchtenthal, Moravia, June
29, 1724. Married Maria E. Minier, in Bethlehem, in 1762, who died in
1769. In 1782 he married Maria Schulz, m.n. Dominick.

256. **Anna Maria Otto**, m.n. Horsfield. xi, n. 3. Dec. 19. Born on Long Island, Aug. 17, 1747. Married Dr. Joseph Otto, in Bethlehem, Jan. 28, 1774. Later they moved to Nazareth. Two of her children survived : Thomas and Anna Maria.

1798.

257. **Johann Gottfried Meyer.** vi, s. 16. March 10. A pupil in Nazareth Hall. Born in St. Croix, W.I., Dec. 22, 1786. His parents were Christian and Jane (Krause) Meyer.

258. **Peter Goetje.** xii, s. 9. March 29. Widower in Christianspring. Born May 2, 1716, at St. Margarethen, Holstein. Married May 27, 1743, in Herrnhaag, Anna Barbara Fleischel, who died in Nazareth, Mar. 15, 1769.

259. **Anna Maria Worbass**, m.n. Schemel. xi, n. 4. April 24. Born Jan. 19, 1722, in Würtemberg. Married Peter Worbass in Bethlehem, July 11, 1758. Two sons, Joseph and Peter, survived.

260. **David Zeisberger.** xiv, s. 1. May 17. Presbyter-Pastor at Nazareth and member of Provincial Board. Born May 25, 1730, in Herrnhut. Married, in Herrnhut, Anna Dorothea Klos.

261. **John David Miksch.** vii, s. 17. Aug. 4. A child; son of John Christian and Anna P. (Loesch) Miksch.

1799.

262. **Christoph Gideon Myrtetus.** xii, s. 10. March 25. Born in Lautern, July 5, 1721. Married Elizabeth Ramstein, Sept., 1754. Three children survived : Elizabeth, married to Jacob Ritter, in Philadelphia, Christopher and John.

263. **Melchior Schmidt.** xii, s. 11. Nov. 23. Born in Zauchtenthal, Moravia, June 4, 1721. Married, in Bethlehem, July 15, 1749, to Catharine Marg. Fischer, who died Aug. 17, 1797. His daughter, Julianna, married John Beitel, Sr., of Nazareth.

1800.

264. **Jacob Stotz.** xiii, s. 8. Jan. 15. Unmarried. (Christianspring.) Born Oct. 19, 1748, in Lauffen, Würtemberg.

265. **Maria Elizabeth Proske.** xiv, n. 1. March 22. Infant daughter of George and Maria Elizab. (Frey) Proske.

266. **Edward Henry.** iii, s. 17. April 6. Infant son of William and Sabina (Schropp) Henry.

267. **John Jacob Eyerly.** xii, s. 12. May 11. Born Jan. 6, 1757, in Old Nazareth. Married, Jan. 13, 1786, to Anna Maria Frey. Five children survived.

268. **Peter Christ.** xii, s. 13. Aug. 20. Died in consequence of a fall from the roof of a house. Born March 25, 1743, in Lauffen, Würtemberg. Married June 18, 1775, to Anna Juliana Herbach. Of his five children, two survived, viz : Jacob, born in Lititz, and Anna Juliana. Married, a year after the death of his wife, to Sarah Kunkler.

1801.

269. **Gottfried Miksch.** vii, s. 18. Feb. 26. Infant son of John Christian and Anna P. Miksch.

270. **John Jacob Vognitz.** vi, s. 17. April 30. Infant son of Fred. Balthazar and Sarah C. (Klein) Vognitz. Small-pox.

271. **Beatus Christ.** vi, s. 18. July 1. Infant son of John and Elizabeth (Grosch) Christ.

272. **Nicholas Fleisner.** xiii, s. 9. July 24. Unmarried. (Christianspring.) Born Sept. 23, 1720, in Saxony. Died in consequence of a broken leg.

273. **Anna Henry.** ii, n. 12. Aug. 22. Daughter of William and Sabina Henry. Aged 16 years.

1802.

274. **Rebecca Youngberg,** m.n. Nixon. xi, n. 5. Feb. 25. Born in Philadelphia, March 10, 1746. Married, April 20, 1775, John Youngberg in Bethlehem.

275. **Maria Catharine Lischer,** m.n. Loesch. xi, n. 6. May 10. Born in Tulpehocken, Pa. Her parents were George and Anna Christina (Wallborn) Loesch. Married, April 16, 1759, in Bethlehem, John Lischer.

276. **John George Hartmann.** xii, s. 14. June 13. (Gnadenthal.) Born in Bischoffsheim, Palatinate. Married Maria Christina Bauss. One daughter survived, viz: Rosina, who married Henry Brunner. In 1775 he married the widow, Susannah Cath. Berndt, who died in 1791

277. **John Adam Huth.** xiii, s. 10. July 28. Unmarried. (Christianspring.) Born Sept. 28, 1737, in Hanau, Germany. He lost an arm in the fight and massacre at Hoeth's on the Pohopoko, in 1755, and barely escaped with his life.

278. **Sarah Stotz.** v, n. 1. Aug. 3. Infant daughter of Joseph and Anna Juliana (Eigenbrod) Stotz.

279. **Heinrich Christoph Loether.** xiii, s. 11. Sept. 17. Unmarried. Born in Perleberg, Brandenburg. Aged 83 years.

280. **Philip Jacob Reizenbach.** xi, s. 18. Sept. 22. A deacon of the Church. Born in Regensburg, Germany, Feb. 28, 1725. Came to America in 1770. In 1779 married Maria Elizabeth Spohn, in Nazareth. Ordained by Bishop John Fr. Reichel, a Deacon of the Church and served as minister in various congregations.

1803.

281. **Beatus Stadiger.** v, s. i. March 21. Son of John Fred. and Susannah Elizabeth (Bagge) Stadiger.

282. **George Schmidt.** xii, s. 15. June 4. A deacon of the Church. Born in Markstett, Nov. 17, 1719. United with the Brethren's Church in 1742. In 1761, he was ordained a deacon of the Church, in Herrnhut. Served as minister in Ireland, and since 1787 in this country, at Gnadenhütten on the Mahony. On account of impaired health, retired in 1796, and moved to Bethlehem, and later to Nazareth. At Cootehill, Ireland, he married Sarah Martin, Nov. 20, 1769. He had one son, who died in Kilwarlin, Ireland.

1804.

283. **John Michael Kern.** xiv, s. 2. May 15. Born in Ebersdorf, Upper Lusatia, June 5, 1750. He married Anna Maria Stoll, in Nazareth, Jan. 17, 1781. He had seven children, of whom three survived: John Christian, Anna Johanna and Andrew Gottfried.

284. **Beata Schweishaupt.** v, n. 2. Aug. 25. Daughter of Joseph and Rosina (Busch) Schweishaupt.

285. **John Jacob Schmick.** xii, s. 16. Oct. 2. Born in Bethlehem, Oct. 2, 1757. Married, in Bethlehem, Feb. 9, 1785, to Anna Johanna Krause. One daughter, Sarah, was married to John S. Haman, of Nazareth.

286. **Catharine Miksch,** m.n. Busch. xi, n. 7. Dec. 27. Born Aug. 14, 1762, in York, Pa. Married Paul Miksch, in Christianspring, March 6, 1796. One son, John Matthew, survived, who became a prominent citizen of Bethlehem.

1805.

287. **Maria Agnes Roth,** m.n. Pfingstag. xi, n. 8. Feb. 25. Born April 4, 1785, in Würtemberg. She came to America in 1737, with her parents, John Michael and Rosina (Ketschle) Pfingstag. Married the Rev. John Roth and served in the Indian missions in western Pennsylvania and Ohio, and later in the pastorates of various Brethren's congregations. Her husband died at York, Pa., on July 19, 1790. Their children were: John, the first white child born in Ohio; John Lewis, John David and John Benjamin. Descendants are prominent laborers in the Lutheran Church.

288. **Juliana Mueller.** i, n. 1. March 23. An unmarried sister. Born in Nazareth, July 27, 1752. Her father was John Bernhard Mueller, who died in Bethlehem, in 1754.

289. **John Jacob Christ.** xii, s. 17. April 2. Born in Lauffen, Würtemberg, Oct. 7, 1740. Came to America, in 1750, with his parents, Rudolph and Anna (Wolfer) Christ. Married, Oct. 25, 1771, Christina Fredericka Schlosser, in Bethlehem. He was a hatter for many years. He had six children, of whom the following survived: Jacobina Fredericka (born Sept. 29, 1772), married to Henry Christian Mueller, a hatter; Christiana (Jan. 19, 1775), married to Joseph Leinbach, a tailor, in Bethlehem; Johanna Maria (June 25, 1778), married to Andrew Benade, Episc. Fratrum; John Jacob (June 3, 1781), a hatter in Nazareth.

290. **Sybilla Barbara Beck,** m.n. Knauer. xi, n. 9. July 2. Born in Pfullingen, Würtemberg, March 24, 1719. In 1738 came, with her parents, to Georgia. Nov., 1738, married Ferdinand Henry Beck, a baker, who died in Bethlehem, in 1783. Of her nine children, three survived: Maria Christina, born in Georgia, Oct. 6, 1739; married Ernst Walther in Bethlehem; later married Michael Ruch, in Christianspring. Christian Henry, born July 17, 1757, in Bethlehem; married Anna Christina Eyerly; Anna Sybilla, born May 11, 1760, in Philadelphia; married John Kremser.

291. **Hans Petersen.** xiii, s. 12. Aug. 22. Unmarried. Born Feb. 21, 1755, in Ostruz, Holstein. Came to America in 1786.

292. **Edward Justus Fuchs.** v, s. 2. Sept. 2. Infant son of John George and Hannah (Warner) Fuchs.

293. **Beatus Christ.** v, s. 3. Nov. 29. Child of John and Elizab. (Grosch) Christ.

1806.

294. **Maria Kunz,** m.n. Dominick. xi, n. 10. Jan. 13. (Gnadenthal.) Born Sept. 11, 1725, in Lower Silesia. Her father died when she was four years old. Married Gottfried Schulz in Bethlehem, July 15, 1749. Of seven children, three sons survived: Gottfried, who moved to North Carolina; John, living in Nazareth; Samuel, who moved to North Carolina. Her husband died in

1779. In 1782 married John David Kunz, who was born in Zauchtenthal, Moravia, and died in Gnadenthal, Dec., 1797.

295. **Andreas Busse.** xiv, s. 3. Jan. 22. Deacon of the Church, and pastor of the church at Nazareth and member of the Provincial Board. Born Dec. 6, 1734, in Reval, Livonia. Married Sept. 9, 1795, Anna Christina Busch. Two children survived : Anna Rosina, married Wm. Rauch, of Lititz, and Christian David.

296. **Melchior Christ.** xii, s. 18. Feb. 24. Born in Lauffen, Würtemberg, Sept. 12, 1734. Came to America with his parents, Rudolph and Anna (Wolfer) Christ, in 1750. Married Maria Barbara Kling, at Lititz, Sept. 19, 1771. Three children survived : John, born in Lititz, July 9, 1772, married Elizabeth Grosch. Maria, married John Clewell.

297. **Peter Worbass.** xiv, s. 4. Sept. 11 Born in Jutland, May 18, 1722. Married Anna Maria Schemel, in Bethlehem, July, 1758. Only one son survived: Joseph, who married Phoebe Hull. He was one of the few who escaped at the massacre at Gnadenhütten on the Mahony.

298. **Beatus Christ.** v, s. 4. Sept. 26. Infant son of John Jacob and Benigna Elizabeth (Ebert) Christ.

299. **Benigna Elizabeth Christ,** m. n. Ebert. xi, n. 11. Sept. 29. Born in Bethlehem, Oct. 17, 1784. Married John Jacob Christ, Nov. 25, 1805.

300. **Anna Philippina Miksch,** m.n. Loesch. xi, n. 12. Oct. 12. Born in Bethabara, North Carolina, April 2, 1763. Married John Christian Miksch, March 19, 1786. Of her eight children, three survived : Jacob, born in Christiansspring, Aug. 24, 1787 ; Rosina, born Aug. 2, 1791 ; Joseph (twin son), Aug. 2, 1796.

301. **Christina Elizabeth Fritz,** m.n. Loesch. xi, n. 13. Nov. 22. Born in Tulpehocken, Pa , Jan. 26, 1733. Her parents were George and Anna Christina (Wallborn) Loesch. In 1759 married Jacob Van der Merk in Bethlehem. Her husband died in Bethabara, N. C., 1772. In 1774, married the Rev. John Christoph Christian Fritz, who died in Gnadenhütten on the Mahony, 1805.

302. **John Jacob Swihel.** xiv, s. 5. Dec. 24. Born in Zittau, Upper Lusatia, July 30, 1737, his parents having fled thither from Bohemia, on account of religious persecution. In 1779 came to America. Married Anna Bryzelius in Nazareth, June 21, 1779. He had two children who died in Emmaus. His wife died, Sept., 1786, in the West Indies, where he was a missionary. Married Anna Rosina Partsch, in Bethlehem, Feb. 24, 1787.

1807.

303. **Mary Magdalena Dealing,** m.n. Graff. vi, n. 13. March 28. Born April 2, 1742, in Lancaster, Pa. In 1779 married John Dealing, who died in Nazareth, Sept. 10, 1785.

304. **John Nicholas Schaefer.** xiv, s. 6. April 12. Born in the state of New York, March 7, 1722. Married Johanna Ysselstein, in Bethlehem, Dec. 25, 1746. Two children survived.

305. **Abraham Reinke.** xiii, s. 13. April 24. Unmarried. A teacher in Nazareth Hall ; died of consumption. Born in York, Pa., Sept. 2, 1787, where his parents, Abraham and Maria Sophia (Rudolph) Reinke, had charge of the congregation.

306. **Lisetta Roth.** v, n. 3. Aug. 31. Infant of John and Susannah Roth.
307. **William Lister.** xiii, s. 14. Sept. 10. Unmarried. Born in Yorkshire, England, Sept. 27, 1715. *Schneidermeister* and *Vorsteher* in the Nazareth Brethren's House. 92 years old.
308. **Beata Senseman.** v, n. 4. Sept. 25. Daughter of Christian David and Anna (Ritter) Senseman.
309. **Maria Christina Ruch,** m.n. Beck. vii, n. 13. Oct. 23. Born Oct. 6, 1739, in Georgia. Married Dietrich Ernst Walther in Bethlehem, Dec. 18, 1767. Her husband died Nov. 26, 1769. Married Michael Ruch, Oct. 25, 1771, who died May 9, 1797.
310. **Anna Margaretha Conradine Strubel.** i, n. 2. Nov. 10. Assistant to the Warden of the Sisters' House. Born in Ungershausen, Würtemberg. Her father was a Lutheran minister, who died six months after her birth. Her mother married another minister, Casper Kerchner. She died during her voyage to America, when her daughter was in her seventh year.

1808.

311. **John Joachim Koepke.** xiii, s. 15. March 3. Unmarried. Born Feb. 6, 1751, in Brandenburg.
312. **George Thomas Graeff.** xiii, s. 16. May 11. Pupil in Nazareth Hall, aged 14 years. Born in Lancaster, Pa. Parents : George and Eva Graeff.
313. **Matthew Krause.** xiv, s. 7. Sept. 5. Farmer in Old Nazareth. Born in Nazareth, May 27, 1747. Married Anna Benigna Partsch, May 15, 1781. He had three sons, one of whom survived him : viz., John Samuel (born June 23, 1782, in Christianspring), a silversmith and watchmaker in the Brethren's House in Bethlehem.
314. **Sarah Catharine Vognitz,** m.n. Klein. ix, n. 13. Sept. 9. Born in Plainfield, Northampton County, Pa., June 25, 1773. Baptized in Schoeneck. On May 29, 1796, she married Frederick B. Vognitz, a brewer and distiller in Christianspring.

1809.

315. **Thomas Tresse Singer.** xiii, s. 17. March 10. Pupil in Nazareth Hall, aged 12 years. Born in Philadelphia. Parents, Abraham and Anna Singer.
316. **Johann Daniel Schweishaupt.** v, s. 5. July 19, Infant son of Joseph and Rosina (Busch) Schweishaupt.

1810.

317. **Benjamin Rudolph Reinke.** v, s. 6. Jan. 9. Pupil in Nazareth Hall. Died of consumption, aged 9 years. Parents, Abraham and Maria Sophia (Rudolph) Reinke.
318. **Peter Kunkler.** xiv, s. 8. Jan. 18. Tailor and teacher near Gnadenthal. Born Dec. 28, 1762, in Bethlehem. In 1791 married Anna Elizabeth Daniel. Of his ten children eight survived their father.
319. **Samuel Miksch.** v, s. 7. Feb. 17. Infant son of Paul and Maria Elizabeth (Rothrock) Miksch.
320. **Christine Clewell.** i, n. 3. April 6. Unmarried sister. Born in Plainfield Township. Her father, Franz Clewell, died in 1798. Aged 47 years.

321. **Anna Maria Gold**, m.n. Roth. viii, n. 13. July 28. Widow. Born in Losswiz, Silesia, Oct. 3, 1725. Married George Gold, in Bethlehem, July 15, 1749. Husband died in 1792.

322. **Edward Henry Huebener.** v, s. 8. Oct. 6. Infant son of Anton and Maria Salome (Knauss) Huebener.

323. **Susanna Fredericka Danke.** v. n. 5. Oct. 12. Daughter of John Frederick and Barbara (Ehrenhardt) Danke.

324. **Laetitia Angelica Fuchs.** xiv, n. 2. Oct. 14. Daughter of John George and Hannah (Warner) Fuchs.

325. **Anna Joanna Boehmer.** i, n. 4. Nov. 4. Unmarried sister. Died of consumption ; aged 60 years. Born in Nazareth, Nov. 4, 1750. Daughter of Martin and Anna Marg. (Essig) Boehmer.

326. **Johannes Hatnick.** xiv, s. 9. Nov. 6. Born in Guttau, near Bautzen, Upper Silesia. Married Elizabeth Hancke, May 31, 1807.

1811.

327. **Anna Maria Busch**, m.n. Wagner. xi, n. 14. Sept. 17. Born April 9, 1728, in Essenheim, Palatinate. Married, 1747, John Louis Spies, who died during the voyage to America. A daughter survived the father. In 1749, married John Busch, a farmer, near York, Pa. Of the eleven children of this union, seven survived.

328. **Johannes Jag.** xiv, s. 10. Nov. 24. Born in Zauchtenthal, Moravia. Married, Oct. 12, 1779, Barbara Holder, in Nazareth. Aged 81 years.

329. **Christina Fredericka Margaretha Christ**, m. n. Schlosser. xi, n. 15. Dec. 16. Born in Pfortsheim, Germany, Feb. 20, 1744. Oct. 25, 1771, married John Jacob Christ, who died April 2, 1805.

1812.

330. **Salome Clewell**, m.n. Kichline. xi, n. 16. May 18. Born Jan. 15, 1728, in Baden. Married, Sept., 1744, Franz Clewell, who died 1798. She had thirteen children.

331. **Anna Christina Krause.** i, n. 5. Sept. 17. An unmarried sister. Born in Nazareth, Oct. 30, 1745.

332. **Beata Brunner.** v, n. 6. Dec. 4. Daughter of John Jacob and Maria Salome (Beitel) Brunner.

1813.

333. **Isaac Renatus Van Vleck.** xiii, s. 18. Oct. 25. Unmarried brother. Son of Henry and Elizabeth (Kreiter) Van Vleck. Born in Lititz, May 24, 1793.

334. **Peter Wolle.** xiv, s. 11. Nov. 20. Missionary to the West Indies. Born in Schwersens, Poland, Nov. 6, 1745. Married Anna Rosina Geier, March 6, 1783. He had five children, of whom the following survived : John Frederick, Jacob Christian, both born in St. Jan ; Peter, born in St. Thomas ; Samuel Henry, in St. Jan. A daughter died in infancy. The sons were prominent in the Bethlehem congregation, Peter being a Bishop of the Church.

335. **George Wenzeslaus Golkowsky.** xiv, s. 12. Dec. 29. An unmarried man, 88 years old. Born in Bobreck, Upper Silesia, 1725. He was an excellent land surveyor, famous far and wide for the accuracy and reliability of his work.

1814.

336. **Arthur Benjamin Schmidt.** v, s. 9. Jan. 28. Infant son of Dr. Henry Benjamin and Anna Maria (Otto) Schmidt.

337. **Emilie Henrietta Schmidt.** v, n. 7. May 5. Infant daughter of Dr. H. B. Schmidt.

1815.

338. **Catharine Ernst,** m.n. Knauss. ix, n. 14. June 16. Born April 21, 1743, in Salisbury Township, Northampton County. Married Conrad Ernst, Feb. 18, 1766.

339. **Francis Henry Eckensberger.** v, s. 10. Oct. 18. Son of Jacob and Magdalena (Danke) Eckensberger.

340. **Sarah Christ,** m.n. Kunkler. viii, n. 14. Nov. 12. Widow. Born in Nazareth, Jan. 13, 1747. Married Peter Christ, Oct. 1, 1787, who died Aug. 20, 1800.

341. **Magdalene Demuth,** m.n. Schnall. vii, n. 14. Nov. 19. Born in Bethlehem, Aug. 10, 1748. Married Joseph Demuth, Aug., 1787.

342. **Hannah Joseph.** vi, n. 14. Nov. 24. A widowed colored woman. Born June 11, 1722, in Esopus, N.Y. Moved to Bethlehem in 1745. Baptized 1752 (see 128). Husband died 1781. Seven children, of whom two daughters survived: Hannah and Mary; the latter married to Peter Titus.

343. **Sarah Gerlach,** m.n. Deiley. vi, n. 15. Dec. 15. Born June 14, 1782, in Williams Township. Married Traugott Gerlach, Feb. 28, 1814.

1816.

344. **Beatus Brunner.** v, s. 11. Jan. 20. Infant son of Jacob and Maria Salome (Beitel) Brunner.

345. **Lucinda Eliza Senseman.** v, n. 8. Jan. 20. Daughter of Christian David and Anna Elizabeth (Ritter) Senseman. Aged 5 years.

346. **Salome Clewell.** i, n. 6. Feb. 9. Unmarried sister. Born Feb. 2, 1761, in Plainfield ; daughter of Franz and Salome (Kichline) Clewell. Her father died in Schoeneck.

347. **Peter Muecke.** xiv, s. 13. April 30. Farmer. Born in Old Nazareth, May 11, 1747, his parents beirg Matthew and Catharine Muecke. Married Anna Opitz, in Bethlehem, April, 1784. Moved to Hope, N.J., where his wife died the same year. In 1785 married Elizabeth Klotz, m.n. Haller.

348. **Maria Elizabeth Proske,** m.n. Frey. vi, n. 16. May 1. Born in Allemängel, Pa., Jan. 2, 1760. Married John George Proske, 1792.

349. **Samuel Schneider.** xiv, s. 14. May 15. Born in Bethlehem, Nov. 22, 1753; parents, John and Elizabeth Schneider. Married Catharine Schmidt, Feb. 4, 1783. His daughter, Catharine Elizabeth, married George Bardill at Nazareth.

350. **Mary Magdalene Eckensberger,** m.n. Danke. vii, n. 15. Oct. 12. Daughter of Frederick and Anna Maria (Clewell) Danke. Married John Jacob Eckensberger, Oct. 27, 1811. Five children.

1817.

351. **Elizabeth Giersch,** m.n. Gerhard. viii, n. 15. April 12. Born in Tulpehocken, Oct. 10, 1741. Married Christian Giersch, in Bethlehem, June 8, 1772. Husband died in 1797.

352. **John Schultz.** xiv, s. 15. April 16. Unmarried man. Schoeneck. Born in Gnadenthal, Dec. 29, 1757.

353. **Matilda Louisa Beck.** xiv, n. 3. May 24. Daughter of Jacob Ferdinand and Anna Rosina (Levering) Beck.

354. **Maria Bittig,** m.n. Rauschenberger. vii, n. 16. Aug. 28. Born Sept. 5, 1756, in Maguntschi (Emmaus). Married George Bittig, April 22, 1792.

355. **Matilda Henrietta Eckensberger.** v, n. 9. Nov. 16. Child of Jacob Eckensberger.

1818.

356. **Barbara Schnall,** m.n. Rank. viii, n. 16. Jan. 21. Born Dec. 28, 1767, near York, Pa. Married Jacob Schnall, 1790. Six children.

357. **Maria Barbara Christ,** m.n. Kling. ix, n. 15. March 2. Born April 30, 1743, in Lancaster County; 1771, Sept. 19, married Melchior Christ, who died in 1806.

358. **Anna Maria Danke,** m.n. Ehrenhard. ix, n. 16. May 9. Born Sept. 10, 1788, in Emmaus. Married Franz Christian Danke, Feb. 10, 1811.

359. **Conrad Ernst.** xiv, s. 16. June 11. Born June 24, 1735, in Upper Palatinate. In 1766 married Catharine Knauss, who died in 1815.

360. **Henry Brunner.** xiv, s. 17. June 29. Born June 4, 1739, in Alsace. In 1773 married Rosina Hartmann. He had eight children, of whom the following survived their father : Elizabeth, married to John Weber in Bethlehem; Christian, married Sybilla Weinland ; Christina ; Anna Catharine, married Gottfried Belling; John Jacob, married Salome Beitel ; Anna Maria ; Rosina. Aged 79 years.

361. **John Jacob Schnall.** xiv, s. 18. July 10. Born in Bethlehem, Jan. 8, 1761. Married Barbara Rank, June 16, 1790. He had six children : Elizabeth, Anna Maria, Rebecca (married Adam Haman), Louisa, John Jacob, Henrietta Dorothea.

362. **Hedwig Angelica Frueauff.** i, n. 7. Aug. 21. Daughter of John Frederick Frueauff, pastor at Nazareth, aged 14 years.

363. **Elizabeth Muecke,** m.n. Haller. xii, n. 1. Sept. 3. Born in Montgomery County, Pa., May 3, 1747. Married Elias Glotz, who died six years later. In 1785 married the widower, Peter Muecke, who died in 1816.

364. **Christina Elizabeth Eyerly,** m.n. Schwarz. xii, n. 2. Sept. 12. Born in Böttingen, Palatinate, March 15, 1730. Both her parents died during the voyage to America, she being only seven years old. In 1755, Aug. 26, married John Jacob Eyerly, who died in 1790. Of her four children, two survived their mother : Maria Elizabeth, who married Owen Rice, and Anna Christina, who married C. H. Beck.

365. **Anna Johanna Kern.** i, n. 8. Dec. 25. An unmarried sister, aged 31 years.

1819.

366. **Rosina Brunner,** m.n. Hartmann. xii, n. 3. Feb. 23. Born Nov. 1, 1748, in Salisbury Township, Northampton Co., Pa. Married Henry Brunner of Christianspring, June 20, 1773. She had eight children (see 360). Her husband died June, 1818.

367. **Rosina Clewell.** i, n. 9. Aug. 11. An unmarried sister; daughter of John and Anna Johanna (Klein) Clewell. Born in Plainfield. Aged 27 years.

368. **Mary Schropp.** i, n. 10. Nov. 10. An unmarried sister; born in Nazareth, June 20, 1747. Aged 72 years.

1820.

369. **Joseph Otto, M.D.** xv, s. 1. Feb. 2. Physician in Nazareth. Born in Bethlehem, April 4, 1745. Married Anna Maria Horsfield, Jan. 28, 1774. Of his five children, only one daughter survived, viz.: Anna Maria, married to Dr. H. T. Schmidt.

370. **Mary Belling, m.n. Edmonds.** xii, n. 4. June 23. Widow of John Gottfried Belling, tanner in Nazareth. Born July 8, 1758, in Connecticut. In 1763 moved to Gnadenhütten on the Mahony. In 1770 married the widower, J. G. Belling. She had six children, of whom two sons and a daughter survived.

1821.

371. **Hannah.** i, n. 11. March 4. A negro sister. Born in Gnadenthal, May 8, 1761. Moved to Nazareth and nursed her mother until her end in 1815; then lived with Peter and Mary Titus.

372. **Christian Russmeyer Schropp.** xv, s. 2. June 23. An unmarried man; teacher in Nazareth Hall. Born Oct. 7, 1796. His parents were Christian and N. (Russmeyer) Schropp. Died of consumption.

373. **Christina Piesch, m.n. Sprecher.** xii, n. 5. Dec. 22. Born Aug. 21, 1730, in Doros, Switzerland. In 1773 married Andrew Piesch, a merchant. Had two sons, one of whom survived. In 1793 came with her husband and younger son to America, and lived in Lancaster, Pa., where her husband died. Then removed to Philadelphia and in 1819 to Nazareth.

1822.

374. **Maria Theresa Busse, m.n. Reinke.** xii, n. 6. April 19. Born in Lancaster, Jan. 23, 1794, where her father was pastor. Married Christian David Busse, April 24, 1814. Her four children survived.

375. **Anna Maria Miksch, m.n. Fritsch.** xii, n. 7. July 7. Born June 14, 1753, in Nazareth. Married Nathaniel Miksch, May 15, 1781. Three sons and a daughter survived.

376. **Mary Titus.** xii, n. 8. Sept. 9. A married colored woman, wife of Peter Titus. Born Aug. 1, 1766. Married, May 7, 1792, Peter Titus.

377. **Lucretia Eliza Ricksecker.** xiv, n. 4. Dec. 17. Infant daughter of John George and Anna Elizabeth (Beitel) Ricksecker.

1823.

378. **John Renatus Kaske.** xv, s. 3. Feb. 14. Born in Berbice, Surinam, Aug. 4, 1749, where his parents were missionaries. He came, as a child, to Nazareth. In 1762 united with the congregation. Later he went to North Carolina, where he married Anna Eva Heyne. In 1793 removed to Gnadenthal.

379. **Anna Schmick.** i, n. 12. March 12. Unmarried sister. Born Dec. 19, 1785, in Bethlehem. Moved to Nazareth, and in 1807 was teacher in the Girls' School. In 1808 became Assistant to the Warden of the Sisters'

House. In 1811 Warden of the Sisters' House in Bethlehem, and later Laboress (*Pflegerin*) there. In 1822, on account of her health, moved to her mother in Nazareth.

380. **Henry Theodore Miksch.** v, s. 12. Sept. 9. Infant son of Jacob and Catharine (Weinland) Miksch.

381. **John Christian Miksch.** xv, s. 4. Dec. 3. Born July 9, 1752, in Bethlehem. Educated there and at Nazareth. Moved to Christianspring, and later learned the trade of blacksmith at Bethlehem. Married Anna P. Loesch. Of his eight children, two sons and a daughter survived, viz.: Jacob, Rosina (married Henry Beitel), and Joseph. His wife died in 1800. In 1809 married Mar. Cath. Hock, m.n. Wingas. During the latter part of his life he was nearly totally blind.

382. **Elizabeth Towle, m.n. Emerson.** xii, n. 9. Dec. 10. Born in London, Jan. 2, 1762. In 1777 removed to Bedford, where she was received into the congregation. Married Samuel Towle, Jan. 12, 1792. Of her six children, two daughters survived. She served, with her husband, as missionary in Antigua, W. Indies, and later in Gnadenhütten on the Mahony, Old Man's Creek, N.J., and Newport, R. I. They retired to Nazareth.

1824.

383. **Samuel Towle.** xv, s. 5. Jan. 1. (Deacon.) Born in England, Nov. 26, 1757. As unmarried man, served as missionary among the Eskimos. In Jan., 1792, married Elizabeth Emerson, and was ordained a Deacon of the Church. Served for a long time in Antigua, W. I., as missionary, and later as minister in Gnadenhütten on the Mahony, Old Man's Creek, N. J., and Newport, R. I. Retired to Nazareth in 1817. His wife died Dec., 1823. Of his six children, two daughters survived, one of whom married Thomas Wohlfahrt in Salem, N. C.

384. **Julianna Beitel, m.n. Schmidt.** xii, n. 10. Feb. 15. Born in Nazareth, Jan. 3, 1751, her parents being Melchior and Cath. Marg. (Fischer) Schmidt. Received into the congregation, Nov. 18, 1770. Married John Beitel, Feb. 7, 1779. Four children: Christian Frederick, John, Rosina, Anna Elizabeth; the latter married John George Ricksecker.

385. **Lucinda Aurelia Clewell.** xiv, n. 5. Sept. 4. Daughter of Jacob and Anna Rebecca (Seyfried) Clewell.

386. **Maria Catharine Haller.** i, n. 13. Oct. 21. Unmarried sister. Born at Muddy Creek, Aug. 31, 1741. Parents were Henry and Anna Marg. Haller. Came to Bethlehem April 17, 1755, and received into congregation in 1758. 1761 to Lititz, 1779 to Gnadenhütten. Later to Nazareth.

387. **Elizabeth Moehring, m.n. Rauschenberger.** xii, n. 11. Nov. 22. Born, Dec. 1, 1747, near Emmaus. Moved to Bethlehem in 1765. Married to Michael Moehring, April 17, 1775, and moved to Nazareth. Husband died April 30, 1796.

1825.

388. **Joseph Stotz.** xv, s. 6. Jan. 4. Born in Gnadenthal, Nov. 3, 1757. Received into congregation in 1771. He had charge of the brick and tile works. In 1796 married Julianna Eigenbrod. Five children survived: Maria, Anna, Joseph, Timothy and John.

389. **Henry Frederick Siewers.** xv, s. 7. Feb. 4. Missionary. Born in Lehre, near Brunswick, Germany, July 11, 1757. Confirmed in the Lutheran Church in 1770. Came to Herrnhut in 1787, and later was received into the congregation in Niesky. After following his trade, having served for a time in the Diaspora work, he was called to the West Indies, as missionary in 1796, and was married to Anna Eliz. Wagner, who died in 1798. His second wife was Maria Magd. Etticofer, who died two weeks after her marriage. In 1799 married the widow, Dorothea Mary Donath, m.n. Wrang, who had eight children, of whom four sons and a daughter survived. In 1822 he retired to Nazareth. He suffered from a severe fall, dropsy finally causing his death.

390. **William Frederick VanVleck.** v, s. 13. March 18. Infant son of W. Henry and Ann Eliza VanVleck, pastor at Nazareth, and Principal of Nazareth Hall.

391. **Christoph Peissert.** xv, s. 8. March 28. Born May 14, 1762, in Reichenau, Silesia. In 1786 went to Kleinwelka, and there was received into the congregation. In 1787 came to America and lived in Christianspring. In 1791 married Rosina Frevel. He was a farmer in Gnadenthal, Old Nazareth and Nazareth. Of his six children, four survived.

392. **Anna Rosina Beck,** m.n. Levering. xii, n. 12. June 3. Born in Nazareth, March 14, 1792. Married Ferdinand Jacob Beck, Feb. 18, 1816. She had five daughters.

393. **Haus.** xiv, n. 6. June 18. Twin daughter of George and Elizabeth Haus.

394. **Elizabeth Kunkler,** m.n. Ohmensetter. xii, n. 13. July 11. Born near Hope, N. J., Aug. 15, 1796. Married David Kunkler, Nov. 21, 1819. One daughter survived. She came from Bethlehem, to be under the care of a physician and died at Nazareth.

395. **Anna Catharine Schneider,** m.n. Luckenbach. xii, n. 14. Nov. 1. Born in New Goschenhoppen, Bucks Co., Pa., Dec. 30, 1743. Having moved to the neighborhood of Bethlehem, married the widower, Adam Schneider, in 1767. She had five children. 1776 received into the congregation. Husband died April, 1801. In 1805 moved from Lower Saucon to Bethlehem, and in 1819 to Plainfield.

396. **Catharine Sybilla Schmidt,** m.n. Whitesell. xii, n. 15 Dec. 12. Daughter of Andrew Whitesell. She was not a member of the congregation. Born in Plainfield, Jan. 20, 1802. Married John Schmidt in 1818.

1826.

397. **Charles Fredr. Miksch.** v, s. 14. Jan. 6. Infant son of John Fredr. and Elizabeth (Huber) Miksch.

398. **Catharine Elizabeth Schmidt.** xiv, n. 7. Jan. 10. Infant daughter of John and Catharine Schmidt.

399. **Agnes Franke.** ii, n. 13. Feb. 21. Unmarried sister. Born in Nazareth, Oct. 6, 1748. In 1752 moved to Bethlehem, where she united with the congregation in 1761. Removed to her parents in Lititz, and after their death, to Nazareth. She was lame from childhood and blind in one eye. When fifty years old became quite blind.

400. **Carl Gotthold Schweisshaupt.** xv, s. 9. May 8. Unmarried man. Born in Nazareth, Nov. 2, 1805. Confirmed in 1821.

401. **Elizabeth Myrtetus,** m.n. Ramstein. xii, n. 16. June 12. Born July 1, 1731, near Basle, Switzerland. In her thirteenth year she came with her parents to America, living at first in the neighborhood of Bethlehem, then beyond the Blue Mountains. There she married Gideon Myrtetus, and later moved to Philadelphia, where she united with the Brethren's Church. Her husband died in 1799. Since 1808 lived in the Senseman family, her granddaughter, Sister Senseman caring for her. Aged 95 years.

402. **Timothy Rothrock Miksch.** v, s. 15. Aug. 4. Son of Paul and Maria Elizabeth (Rothrock) Miksch.

403. **George Henry Bardill.** v, s. 16. Sept. 28. Son of George Rudolph and Catharine Elizabeth (Schneider) Bardill.

404. **Lavinia Fredericka Busse.** xiv, n. 8. Oct. 18. Infant daughter of Christian David and Mary (Rauch) Busse.

405. **James Edward Ricksecker.** xv, s. 10, Oct. 18. Son of George and Elizabeth (Beitel) Ricksecker. Born Nov. 25, 1811. He was a very talented and studious boy.

406. **Caroline Emilia Kern.** xiv, n. 9. Nov. 5. Infant daughter of Andrew Gottfried and Catharine Louisa (Levering) Kern.

407. **Henry Benjamin Schmidt, M.D.** xv, s. 11. Nov. 24. Born in Brettstadt, Schleswig Holstein, Oct. 1, 1782. As a child he went to Christiansfeld with his widowed mother. In 1790 he entered the Paedagogium in Niesky. Thence he went to Barby to school, and later to a druggist in Gnadenfrei. When 19 years old he entered the University in Jena, and later went to Göttingen. He came to Nazareth, as a physician, in 1804. In 1805, July 21, he married Anna Maria Otto. Of his children, five survived him; viz.: Henry Emanuel, (Professor in New York,) Charlotte Louisa, Maria Caroline (married Brother Wm. L. Lennert), Emma Cornelia (married Brother Julius T. Bechler), and Edward Otto (a sugar refiner in Philadelphia and prominent member of the Church there). During several years he was in poor health, in consequence of attacks of paralysis. He was a skilful and highly esteemed physician and valued member of the congregation.

1827.

408. **Joseph Demuth.** xv, s. 12. Feb. 23. Born in Fredericktown, Dec. 1, 1748. In 1760 came to Bethlehem, then moved to Nazareth. Married Mary Magdalene Schnall, Aug. 15, 1787, who died Nov. 1815.

409. **Caroline Jane Van Vleck.** xiv, n. 10. April 22. Infant daughter of W. Henry and Ann Eliza (Kampmann) Van Vleck.

410. **John Frederick Danke.** xv, s. 13. May 21. Born in Nazareth, Sept. 5, 1780. Superintendent of the shoemaking shop in the Brethren's House. Later he changed his occupation, carrying on a bakery. Married Barbara Ehrenhard of Emmaus, Jan. 10, 1808. Of his seven children, six survived their father: Lisetta Louisa, Mary Ann Theodora, Elfrida Caroline (married Francis Miksch), Julianna Emilie (married Gustav A. Kern), Henrietta Cecilia (married Harvey Bates), and Alfred Henry (a prominent member of the Schoeneck congregation).

411. **James Albright.** xv, s. 14. Sept. 13. Son of Henry and Anna Barbara (Hubley) Albright. Born in Shippensburg, Pa. Moved with his parents, to Gnadenhütten, Ohio, then to Lititz and to Nazareth. United with the Church in 1824. Having gone to Easton to enter business there, was taken ill, and being removed to his home in Nazareth, died there, aged 21 years.

412. **Henry Augustus Ricksecker.** v, s. 17. Sept. 15. Infant son of George and Elizab. (Beitel) Ricksecker.

413. **Dorothea Gold.** ii, n. 14. Nov. 2. Unmarried sister; daughter of George and Anna Maria Gold. Born in Old Nazareth, Aug. 4 1762.

414. **Nathaniel Miksch.** xv, s. 15. Nov. 7. Born in Bethlehem, Sept. 21, 1743. Lived in Fredericktown, Bethlehem (where he united with the congregation), and Christianspring. 1781 married Anna Maria Fritsch, and carried on the milling business at Friedensthal; later occupied a farm between Friedensthal and Nazareth. His wife died July 7, 1822. Of his six children, four survived: John Frederick, Nathaniel, John Christian, and Anna Rebecca (married to Peter Stoudt [Stout]).

415. **Beata Schmidt.** xiv, n. 11. Infant daughter of John and Sophia (Beck) Schmidt.

1828.

416. **Anna Johanna Clewell, m.n. Klein.** xiii, n. 1. Jan. 19. Born in Saucon, Feb. 2, 1760. Parents: Andrew and Jane Elizabeth (Thomas) Klein. Moved to Plainfield, where she became acquainted with the Brethren's Church. Married John Clewell, April 25, 1780, and the same year was baptized and united with the Brethren's Church. In 1793 moved to Nazareth. Of her nine children, eight survived their mother.

417. **Elizabeth Rice.** i, n. 14. Feb. 25. Unmarried sister, daughter of Owen and Elizabeth Rice (minister at Bethlehem). Educated in Bethlehem Seminary. In 1780 went to Nazareth Sisters' House, and became superintendent of the older girls, being received as an acolyte. Aged 79 years.

418. **Louisa Charlotte Clewell.** xiv, n. 12. March 7. Infant daughter of Jacob and Rebecca (Seyfried) Clewell.

419. **Edmund Fairing Trost.** v, s. 18. March 8. Infant son of William and Marg. Trost (non-members) living at Nazareth.

420. **Lydia Schenck,** m.n. Michael. xiii, n. 2. March 20. Daughter of John and Elizabeth (Billmeyer) Michael. Born in Moore Township, Nov. 12, 1802. Married the widower Thomas M. Schenk, 1819. They lived, during their last years, in Old Nazareth, but did not belong to the congregation.

421. **Benjamin Franklin Stotz.** x, s. 1. April 18. Infant son of Joseph and Henrietta (Ernst) Stotz.

422. **John Clewell.** xv, s. 16. April 28. Born in Plainfield Township, April 21, 1750; son of Franz and Salome (Kichline) Clewell. United with the congregation in Schoeneck. Married Anna Johanna Klein, April 25, 1780. Of his nine children, eight survived their father: Elizabeth (married Andrew Whitesell), John, Anna Johanna (married Jacob Eckensberger), Joseph, Anna Catharine, Sarah, Jacob and Thomas. In 1793 moved to a farm at Nazareth. His wife died in 1828.

423. **Anna Catharine Clewell.** ii, n. 15. July 18. Daughter of John and Anna J. (Klein) Clewell. Born Sept. 19, 1790.
424. **Rosina Fritsch.** ii, n. 16. Oct. 29. Unmarried sister. Born July 12, 1762. Parents were Henry and Margaret Fritsch.

1829.

425. **Emma Henrietta Schmick.** xiv, n. 13. Jan. 9. Infant daughter of William and Rosina (Blickensderfer) Schmick.
426. **Anna Christina Busse,** m.n. Busch. xiii, n. 3. April 19. Born in York, Pa., Jan. 4, 1754. Daughter of John and Anna Maria Busch. Came to Lititz, where she united with the congregation. Married Andrew Busse (minister), Sept. 9, 1785, and with him served in Gnadenthal, Old Nazareth and Nazareth. Her husband died Jan. 22, 1806. She had a son and a daughter. Aged 75 years.
427. **Edward Shober Herman.** x, s. 2. Oct. 4. Son of John G. and A. Pauline (Shober) Herman, minister and Principal of Nazareth Hall.
428. **John Weinland.** xv, s. 17. Oct. 28. Born in Old Nazareth, Sept. 3, 1750, son of John Nicholas and Philippine (Loesch) Weinland. He was in the Nazareth nursery until his twelfth year. Then he went to Bethlehem, to learn the saddler's trade. Later he carried on business in Hope, N.J. By an accident, he lost the sight in one eye. Moved to Lititz, then to Philadelphia, where he married Philippine Boemper. After living 35 years on a farm at Hope, N. J., moved to Nazareth in 1813. He had two sons and seven daughters, of whom three daughters died in infancy. Here at Nazareth he was "Fremden Diener" at the Inn.

1830.

429. **Anna Barbara Albright,** m.n. Hubley. xiii, n. 4. Feb. 25. Daughter of Bernhard and Maria Hubley; born at Lancaster, Pa., March 21, 1773. Baptized and confirmed in the Lutheran church. In 1794, March 27, married Henry Albright. United with the congregation at Lititz in 1810. She had ten children; six sons and four daughters.
430. **Louis Edward Miksch.** xv, s. 18. May 12. Son of Jacob and Catharine (Weinland) Miksch. Born May 16, 1813. Went to Bethlehem to learn the coppersmith's trade. Died of consumption. Aged 17 years.
431. **John Frederick Schaefer.** xvi, s. 1. June 22. Born in Gnadenthal, Oct. 28, 1757. Married Anna Rosina Gold, May, 1787. He had three daughters. He was "erster Saaldiener" (chief sexton).
432. **Edward Samuel Haman.** x, s. 3. July 10. Infant son of John S. and Sarah (Schmick) Haman.
433. **Nicholas Elias Hoeber.** xvi, s. 2. Aug. 4. Warden at Nazareth. Born June 4, 1760, in Schleswig. Baptized and confirmed in the Lutheran Church. In 1778, July 10, united with the Brethren's congregation in Zeist, Holland. After the Synod of 1789, he received a call as Brethren's laborer in Nazareth. In 1799 called to Heidelberg, Pa., as minister, and was married, Feb. 14, to Johanna Sophia Lehman, and was ordained as deacon in Lititz. Two years later, he was called to Bethel, as pastor. In 1808 became warden at Nazareth. Two sons survived.

434. **Fredericka Miksch.** i, n. 15. Aug. 28. Daughter of Frederick and Elizabeth (Huber) Miksch. Born May 19, 1814. When nine years old, moved to Lititz to relatives. There united with the congregation. In 1829 returned to Nazareth.

435. **Anna Dorothea Kern,** m.n. Schneider. xiii, n. 5. Sept. 7. Born in Old Nazareth, Nov. 10, 1794; daughter of Samuel and Catharine (Schmidt) Schneider. Married Peter Kern, Aug. 15, 1820. Four children.

436. **Susanna Seyfried,** m.n. Ehrenhard. xiii, n. 6. Sept. 15. Born in Emmaus, Jan. 17, 1759. Married Nicholas Seyfried in Bethlehem, Feb. 28, 1780. Lived several years in the neighborhood of Bethlehem, then at Friedensthal; 1808 at Old Nazareth and later at Nazareth. She had two children. On Feb. 28, 1830, celebrated her "golden wedding."

437. **Ebenezer Leinbach Miksch.** x, s. 4. Oct. 11. Infant son of Nathaniel and Julianna (Leinbach) Miksch.

438. **John Poppelwell.** xvi, s. 3. Oct. 31. Unmarried. Born at Bethlehem, March 28, 1761.

1831.

439. **Philippine Eub.** i, n. 16. Feb. 14. Unmarried sister. Born in Warwick, Oct. 18, 1756. Daughter of Andrew and Christina (Hofman) Eub. Spent her childhood in Graceham, Md. Went to Lititz. In 1769 united with the congregation there. In 1786 moved to Nazareth. She was sick-nurse in the Sisters' House.

440. **Anna Barbara Bardill,** m.n. Mettler. xiii, n. 7. March 16. Born July 15, 1756, in Stoffa, Canton Zurich. Her parents were Rudolph and Rosina Mettler. 1782, received into the congregation at Gnadau. Married John Bardill, Aug., 1787, and they served nearly twelve years as missionaries in Antigua, W. I. Returning to this country on account of impaired health, served in Emmaus and New York, and, for a short time, at Goshen, on the Muskingum, among the Indians, until the station was abandoned. Came to Nazareth. She was paralyzed for several years, a severe fall occasioning death.

441. **Catharine Schneider,** m.n. Schmidt. xiii, n. 8. March 26. Born in Bethlehem, April 23, 1760. Married, Feb. 4, 1783, Samuel Schneider of Old Nazareth, who died May 15, 1816. A son and daughter survived.

442. **Agnes Beata Herman.** xiv, n. 14. May 14. Daughter of John Gottlieb and Anna Paulina (Shober) Herman, pastor and Principal of Nazareth Hall.

443. **John Jacob Schmidt.** x, s. 5. May 27. Infant son of John and Sophia (Beck) Schmidt.

444. **Beata Smith.** xiv, n. 15. Sept. 1.

1832.

445. **Edward Ferdinand Miksch.** x, s. 6. Jan. 15. Infant son of Joshua and Pauline (Stauber) Miksch.

446. **Johanna Maria Shober.** i, n. 17. May 23. Daughter of Nathaniel and Rebecca (Haines) Shober, of Salem, N. C.

447. **Gottfried Sebastian Oppelt.** xvi, s. 4. Aug. 9. Minister. Born May 20, 1763, in Görlitz. As a child, he came to Herrnhut, and later studied in the Paedagogium and Theological Seminary. Served as teacher in Kleinwelka.

Came to Nazareth Hall, as teacher, in 1793. In 1799 ordained by Bishop Ettwein, as Deacon, and on April 4, married Anna Catharine Westhoefer, in Lititz. Went to Fairfield, Canada, as missionary among the Indians. In 1805, removed, with our Indians, to Petquoting and assisted in founding a new station. In 1807, on account of impaired health, was called to Emmaus In 1810, as Agent of the Mission, removed to Muskingum. In 1818 returned to Nazareth.

448. **Anna Johanna Schmick,** m.n. Krause. xiii, n. 9. Aug. 11. Born in Bethlehem, Sept. 29, 1761. Married John Jacob Schmick, Feb. 9, 1785. In 1791 moved to Nazareth. Husband died Oct. 2, 1804.

449. **Jacob Franklin Wilhelm.** x, s. 7. Aug. 26. Infant son of Daniel and Maria (Beck) Wilhelm.

450. **Matthew Cassler.** xvi, s. 5. Sept. 24. Born in Lititz, April 15, 1771. Had left the congregation. Married Margaret Rummage.

451. **Caroline Cecilia Kern.** xiv, n. 16. Sept. 29. Infant daughter of Andrew G. and Louisa (Levering) Kern.

452. **John Nicholas Seyfried.** xvi, s. 6. Oct. 4. Born Oct. 25, 1754, in Alsace. In his fifteenth year, came to America, with his parents, settling in the neighborhood of Bethlehem. United with the congregation at Bethlehem. Married Susanna Ehrenhard, of Emmaus, Feb. 28, 1780. For many years farmer at Friedensthal and Old Nazareth. He had ten children, of whom two sons and four daughters survived. His wife died in 1830.

453. **Lucinda Eliza Kern.** xiv, n. 17. Oct. 7. Infant daughter of Andrew G. and Louisa (Levering) Kern. Died of scarlet fever.

454. **Susan Elmira Deemer.** v, n. 10. Oct. 28. Daughter of John and Susan (Albright) Deemer. Scarlet fever.

1833.

455. **Samuel Levin Seyfried.** x, s. 8. Jan. 5. Son of John and Maria (Eyerly) Seyfried. Scarlet fever.

456. **Mary Ann Kichline.** v, n. 11. Jan. 30. Daughter of Aaron Kichline. Scarlet fever.

457. **Augusta Sophia Busse.** ii, n. 17. April 19. Daughter of Christian David and Maria Theresa (Reinke) Busse. Born Jan. 15, 1817.

458. **Venilia Clementina Folkerson.** v, n. 12. May 30. Daughter of Philip Folkerson and his wife, Christina, m.n. Clewell. Born in Schoeneck, Jan. 19, 1823. Father had died previously. Scarlet fever.

459. **Christian Frederick Beitel.** xvi, s. 7. June 3. Born July 9, 1752, at Pilgerruh, Berbice.

460. **John Dietrich Gottfried Belling.** xvi, s. 8. June 13. Born Sept. 2, 1747, in Grafschaft Mark. Piously reared by his parents. United with the congregation in Zeist, 1768. Came to America in 1770. Lived at Christiansspring, later at Bethlehem, learning the trade of tanner. In 1782 came to Nazareth, where he carried on his trade. Married Rosina Kremser in 1782, who died in 1789. In 1790 married Mary Edmonds, who died in 1820. By his first marriage he had two sons, and by the second six children, of whom four died. During last years of his life he lived with his son Gottfried Belling, near Nazareth.

461. **Christina Folkerson**, m.n. Clewell. xiii, n. 10. July 15. Born in Schoeneck, Oct. 11, 1796. In 1816 united with the congregation. Married Philip Folkerson in 1818. Her husband died in 1824. She had two sons and a daughter.

462. **Christian Henry Miller.** xvi, s. 9. Sept. 17. Merchant. Born March 2, 1767, in Sachse Meinungen. When fourteen years old, united with the congregation in Ebersdorf. He was a hatter by trade. Later went to Christiansfeld. In 1793 came to America, and worked as hatter for Brother Christ. Married Jacobina Fredericka Christ in 1795. The same year he assumed the management of the newly established store of the congregation. In 1829 bought the same, carrying it on in his own name. Died unexpectedly.

463. **Anna Christina Beck**, m.n. Eyerly. xiii, n. 11. Nov. 21. Born in Nazareth, Jan. 27, 1764. Received into the congregation in 1781. In 1790 married the widower Christian Henry Beck, living in Christianspring till 1800. She had two sons and five daughters, of whom one son and four daughters survived.

1834.

464. **Caroline Louisa Moore.** v, n. 13. Jan. 12. Infant daughter of Dr. Peter Moore and his wife, Henrietta, m.n. Kluge.

465. **Anna Gambold.** x, n. 1. Jan. 19. Unmarried sister. Born at Old Man's Creek, N. J., Feb. 9, 1756, where her parents, Hector and Eleonora Gambold, served as ministers. In 1759 came to Bethlehem School. 1783 moved to Sisters' House at Nazareth, where she was accountant. In consequence of a severe fall, she suffered greatly.

466. **Christian Stauber Beck.** x, s. 9. Jan. 20. Son of Ferd. Jacob and Caroline L. Beck.

467. **Maria Magdalena Clewell.** iii, n. 13. April 13. Infant daughter of John Gottfried and Judith (Everett) Clewell.

468. **John George Ricksecker.** xvi, s. 10. May 2. Tailor. Born in Lititz, Dec. 14, 1782. Moved to Hope, N. J., where his father died. Then came to Bethlehem, where he united with the congregation. Later to Nazareth. Nov. 11, 1810, married Anna Elizabeth Beitel. One son and one daughter survived.

469. **William Augustus Kern.** x, s. 10. May 14. Infant son of Peter and Charlotte (Pietsch) Kern.

470. **John Gottfried Clewell.** xvi, s. 11. June 25. Born in Schoeneck, July 12, 1802. Later, worked at his trade as wagoner, in Lebanon, then at Bethlehem. Married Judith Everett of Emmaus, in 1826, May 23, and moved to Nazareth. Two daughters survived.

471. **Anna Rosina Werner.** x, n. 2. July 28. Unmarried sister. Born in Bethlehem, Oct. 28, 1755, daughter of John William and Anna Maria (Shugarth) Werner. In 1763 moved, with her parents, to Lititz, uniting with that congregation. 1780 moved into the Nazareth Sisters' House. In 1784 into the new building.

472. **Anna Bauer.** x, n. 3. July 31. Unmarried sister. Born in Usingen, Würtemberg, Dec. 4, 1746. In 1752 came with her parents, Martin and Anna Bauer, to America. In 1762 all united with the congregation in Emmaus. In 1766 moved to Nazareth. 1784 into the new Sisters' House.

473. **Augusta Christina Wilhelm.** iii, n. 14. Aug. 6. Infant daughter of Daniel and Maria (Beck) Wilhelm.

474. **Anna Pauline Herman.** iii, n. 15. Aug. 7. Infant daughter of Rev. J. G. and Anna P. (Shober) Herman.

475. **Sarah Ann Haman.** x, n. 4. Aug. 8. Daughter of John S. and Sarah (Schmick) Haman. Born April 11, 1819. She was an invalid from her birth, mentally and bodily.

476. **Jacob Frederick Hillman.** x, s. 11. Aug. 11. Infant son of Joseph and Anna Christina Hillman.

477. **Araminta Louisa Miller.** iii, n. 16. Aug. 22. Infant daughter of Charles and Anna Johanna Miller.

478. **Benjamin Franklin Ricksecker.** x, s. 12. Nov. 11. Son of Samuel and Anna Justina Ricksecker. (An epidemic of dysentery prevailed.)

479. **Elizabeth Schaefer.** x, n. 5. Nov. 28. Unmarried sister.

480. **Frederick Jacob Schmidt.** xvi, s. 12. Dec. 1. Unmarried man. Born in Bethlehem, Aug. 6, 1758. United with Nazareth congregation in 1775. Lived in Christianspring, and later was cook in the Brethren's House in Nazareth. He was very liberal in his contributions to missions. Taught boys and young men gratuitously in the evening.

481. **Christian David Senseman.** xvi, s. 13. Dec. 13. Merchant. Born May 30, 1781, at Schoenbrunn, on the Muskingum, where his parents were missionaries. When three days old, he was taken, with his parents, to Sandusky, by enemies of the mission. When six years old he entered Nazareth Hall as a pupil. When fourteen years old, he was employed in the store of the congregation. Married Anna Elizabeth Ritter, in Philadelphia, Nov. 27, 1806. He had five sons and two daughters, the latter dying in childhood.

482. **William Hessler.** xvi, s. 14. Dec. 22. Born in Bethlehem, Nov. 9, 1753. Educated in Nazareth Hall. When thirteen years of age, went to Christianspring to learn weaving. Later, moved to Bethlehem, Lititz, etc. In 1788 moved to Hope, N. J., and married Hannah Brown, who died a few years later. In 1794 married Mary Magdalene Koehler, in Lititz. Continued to live in Hope until 1808, when he moved to Nazareth. One son survived.

1835.

483. **Maria Catharine Miksch,** m.n. Wingass. xiii, n. 12. Jan. 16. Born near Elberfield, Westphalia. Married George Hoeck. Of five children, only one daughter, Catharine, survived her mother. On the journey to America, her husband died in Holland. Her other four children having died, and having lost all her possessions, she came to Gnadenthal. In 1809 she married John Christian Miksch, who died in 1823. Her age was 70 years.

484. **Christian Samuel Michael.** xvi, s. 15. March 1. Born Nov. 10, 1767, in Kienhausen, near Erfurt. As musician, served his time in Barby. Came to America in 1795, with his brother Moritz, and united with the congregation in Nazareth. He became a skillful carpenter. Married Elizabeth Giersch, March 2, 1800. He had two sons and two daughters.

485. **Anna Maria Danke,** m.n. Clewell. xiii, n. 13. March 24. Born June 24, 1752, in Plainfield. In 1773 confirmed in Schoeneck. Married Frederick Danke, Oct. 12, 1779. She had three sons and a daughter. Her husband died April 18, 1793.

486. **Anna Maria Segner.** x, n. 6. April 26. An unmarried sister. Born in Bethlehem, Dec. 13, 1745, where her parents were on a visit from the West Indies. In 1780 moved to Nazareth, and in 1784 into the new Sisters' House.

487. **Beatus Kern.** x, s. 13. June 6. Son of Peter and Charlotte Kern.

488. **Beatus Matzenbacher.** x, s. 14.

489. **Beata Roth.** iii, n. 17.

490. **Emilius Walter.** x, s. 15. Oct. 25. Son of Dr. Philip and Rachel B. (Sellers) Walter. Born Nov. 19, 1825. Fell from a tree and was fatally injured.

491. **Philippine Weinland,** m.n. Boemper. xiii, n. 14. Dec. 12. Born at Hoeth's settlement on the Pohopoko Creek, (the scene of the massacre in 1755, and later the site of the Indian Mission Station, Wechquetank,) Nov. 14, 1753. Lived in the Sisters' House at Bethlehem, then in Philadelphia, where she married John Weinland. With him she moved to Hope, N. J., and, in 1813, to Nazareth. Her husband died Oct., 1829. Of her nine children, six survived. She had forty-nine grand children and thirty-six great-grandchildren.

492. **George Proske.** xvi, s. 16. Dec. 20. Born in Upper Silesia, Jan. 1, 1748. In 1768 went to Herrnhut, then to Zeist, where he united with the congregation. During several years he was engaged at the mill in Sarepta, Russia. Later came to Christianspring. Married Maria Elizabeth Frey, in May, 1792. She died in 1816. Two sons and a daughter survived.

1836.

493. **Margaret Cassler,** m.n. Rummage. xiii, n. 15. Jan. 10. Widow of Matthew Cassler.

494. **Theophilus Walter Miksch.** x, s. 16. Feb. 8. Infant son of Christian Aug. and Mary Ann (Walter) Miksch.

495. **Paul Miksch.** xvi, s. 17. March 14. A Deacon of the Church. Born Nov. 18, 1763, in Bethlehem. Educated at Nazareth Hall, then learned the trade of blacksmith. Served in Christianspring as the Superintendent (Pfleger) of the unmarried brethren, and as warden in Gnadenthal. In 1795 married Catharine Busch. In 1802 ordained a Deacon by Bishop Loskiel. His wife died Dec. 27, 1804. In 1806 married Maria Elizabeth Rothrock. One son, J. M. Miksch, (a prominent citizen of Bethlehem and member of the Church there) was the only surviving child of the first marriage. Of the second, two sons and two daughters survived.

496. **Rosina Clewell.** x, n. 7. March 16. An unmarried sister. Born Sept. 29, 1759, in Plainfield. Daughter of Franz and Salome Clewell.

497. **Harriet Trost.** iv, n. 14. March 26. Born Nov. 2, 1833.

498. **Rachel Simmons Trost.** iv, n. 13. March 28. Born March 10, 1836.

499. **Joseph Theodore Hoeber.** x, s. 17. April 16. Son of Christian R. and Rebecca (Clewell) Hoeber.

500. **Beatus Oppelt.** x, s. 18. June 2. Infant son of Francis and Louisa Oppelt.

501. **Beata Wilhelm.** iv, n. 15. June 6. Infant daughter of Daniel and Maria Wilhelm.

502. **Catharine Salome Sherer.** x, n. 8. Aug. 22. An unmarried sister. Born Sept. 13, 1756, at Zweibruecken. Came, as a child, with her parents to America. Suffered greatly from cancer in the face.

1837.

503. **Catharine Louisa Kern**, m.n. Levering. xiii, n. 16. Jan. 13. Born in Nazareth, June 4, 1793. Married Andrew Gottfried Kern, Feb. 21, 1819. She had eight children, of whom five survived.

504. **Andrew Albright**. xvi, s. 18. Feb. 23. Son of Henry and Anna Barbara (Hubley) Albright. Born in Shippensburg, Cumberland Co., Pa., March 28, 1802. Later moved to Nazareth. In 1816 united with the Church. After some time spent in Lancaster, engaged in business, came here and lived in Moorestown. Oct. 16, 1823, married Agnes Dunn. He had four sons and a daughter.

505. **Edwin S. Trost**. xvii, s. 1, Feb. 25.

506. **Theodore Emanuel Clewell**. xvii, s. 2. March 9. Infant son of Benjamin and Augusta (Rondthaler) Clewell.

507. **Jacob Bininger**. xviii, s. 1. April 11. Pupil in Nazareth Hall, in the class preparing for the Theological Seminary. Son of Jacob and Harriet Bininger. Born in New York, Feb. 2, 1822.

508. **Maria Dorothea Warner**. x, n. 9. April 24. Unmarried sister. Born in Philadelphia, Feb. 5, 1818. Her parents were John and Martha (McGilton) Warner. Came to Bethlehem in her sixth year. Confirmed April 4, 1833. She was assistant teacher for small girls in Bethlehem until, on account of illness and melancholy, she was obliged to go to her parents in Christiansspring.

509. **Anna Rosina Christ**. x, n. 10. July 3. Unmarried sister. Born in Friedensthal, April 3, 1752. Daughter of Rudolph and Anna Christ. Being diseased in body and mind, removed to Brother and Sister Hanke in Ephrata. Aged 85 years.

510. **Lewis Frederick Ricksecker**. xviii, s. 2. July 8. Unmarried man. Born Sept. 3, 1819. In 1836 went to Lancaster to learn the trade of plane-maker, with Emanuel Carpenter. Soon returned, as his father needed his assistance. Fatally injured by falling from a horse.

511. **Beatus Weierman**. xvii, s. 3.

512. **Aaron Hillman Michael**. xvii, s. 4. Sept. 2. Infant son of David F. and Phoebe Ann Michael.

513. **Anna Maria Hanke**, m.n. Frey. xiii, n. 17. Nov. 16. Born in Lititz, April 8, 1759. Daughter of Henry Frey. In her second year entered the nursery in Bethlehem. 1784 moved into the Sisters' House in Nazareth. In 1786 married Jacob Eyerle, who died in 1800. She had two sons and three daughters. In 1804 married the widower, Matthias Hanke, and after living for a time in Hope, N. J., returned to Nazareth.

514. **Beatus Stotz**. xvii, s. 5. Dec. 14.

1838.

515. **Agnes Henrietta Dober**. v, n. 14. Jan. 13. Infant daughter of Carl and Wilhelmina Henrietta Benigna (Trautvetter) Dober. Her father was Professor in the Theological Seminary at Nazareth.

516. **Elizabeth Whitesell**, m.n. Clewell. xii, n. 17. Feb. 19. Born in Plainfield, April 16, 1791. In 1817, July 20, married the widower Andrew Whitesell, and in 1818 moved from Mt. Bethel to Old Nazareth. She had two daughters.

517. **Beata Hoeber.** v, n. 15. March 18. Infant daughter of Christian R. and Rebecca Hoeber.

518. **Anna Pauline Dernbach**, m.n. Miksch. xi, n. 17. April 8. Born in Christianspring, April 21, 1808. Married John Michael Dernbach, Oct. 26, 1834.

519. **Christian Henry Dernbach.** xvii, s. 6. May 25. Child.

520. **Anna Maria Seyfried**, m.n. Eyerly. xiii, n. 18. July 27. Born in Nazareth, April 12, 1792, daughter of Jacob and Anna Maria Eyerly. United with congregation in Hope, N.J. Married John Seyfried, March 29, 1813. She had six sons and three daughters.

521. **John Jacob Brunner.** xviii, s. 3. Aug. 7. Born in Old Nazareth, Dec. 10, 1786. Married Salome Beitel, Nov. 17, 1811. Of his six children, one son and three daughters survived.

522. **Anna Eva Kaske**, m.n. Heyne. ix, n. 17. Oct. 5. Born at Broadbay, Maine, July 20, 1756. Received into the congregation at Salem, N.C., in 1777. Married John Renatus Kaske in Gnadenthal, in 1789. Her husband died in 1823.

523. **Beatus Shireman.** xvii, s. 7. Oct. 9. Infant son of Daniel and Selinda (Beitel) Shireman.

524. **Beata Michael.** v, n. 16. Oct. 22. Daughter of David and Phoebe Michael.

525. **Albert Lewis Clewell.** xvii, s. 8. Dec. 6. Infant son of Renatus and Mary Ann (Siess) Clewell.

1839.

526. **Ellen Jane Walter.** iv, n. 16. Jan. 4. Infant daughter of Dr. Philip and Rachel B. (Sellers) Walter.

527. **Caroline Elizabeth Christ.** x, n. 11. March 17. Unmarried sister. Born in Lititz, June 17, 1811. In April, 1830, moved to Nazareth, with her widowed mother, Anna Christ, who became sick-nurse in Nazareth Hall. She lived in the Sisters' House and in 1831 taught in the Girls' School.

528. **Rudolph Hitz.** xvii, s. 9. June 22. Son of John Hitz, consul to United States from Switzerland. The child died while the parents were visiting their son, Hans Hitz, a pupil in Nazareth Hall.

529. **Elizabeth Schnall.** x, n. 12. Sept. 16. Unmarried sister. Daughter of Jacob and Barbara (Rank) Schnall. Born in Old Nazareth, Oct. 29, 1791. After the death of her parents, she lived in the Sisters' House.

1840.

530. **Beatus Michael.** xvii, s. 10. Jan. 20. Infant son of David and Phoebe Michael.

531. **Edwin Samuel Kichline.** xvii, s. 11. May 24. Infant son of Conrad and Eloisa Kichline.

532. **Juliana Stotz**, m.n. Eigenbrod. viii, n. 17. June 13. Born near Graceham, Md., Feb. 12, 1766. In 1783 moved to Lititz, and there received into the congregation. Married Joseph Stotz of Nazareth, Dec., 1796. She had three sons and three daughters, of whom one daughter died in infancy. After the death of her husband, in Jan., 1825, she lived in Schoeneck, with her daughter, Mrs. George Beitel.

533. **John Beitel.** xviii, s. 4. Sept. 27. Born in Pilgerhut, near Berbice River, Surinam, where his parents, Henry and Elizabeth Beitel, were missionaries. In his fifth year he was brought to America, entering the school then existing in Fredericktown, Montgomery Co., Pa. When this was discontinued, he moved to Emmaus, remaining there two years. In 1752 went to Bethlehem. 1756 to Christianspring, then to Bethlehem, etc. In 1771 united with the congregation at Nazareth. Married Juliana Schmidt in 1779. He had four children, two sons and two daughters. His wife died Feb. 15, 1824. His age was 100 years, less 84 days.

534. **Emma Elizabeth Kern.** xiv, n. 18. Dec. 15. Infant daughter of Andr. Gottfried and Sarah (Lichtenthaeler) Kern.

1841.

535. **Thaddeus McAlpine.** xviii, s. 5. Jan. 17. Pupil in Nazareth Hall. Born Nov. 17, 1825, in Mobile, Alabama.

536. **Beata Seyfried.** iv, n. 17. Jan. 30. Infant daughter of Joseph and Antoinette (Miksch) Seyfried.

537. **Christian Benjamin Whitesell.** xviii, s. 6. Jan. 30. Came from Newark, N. J. Son of Andrew Whitesell. Born in Plainfield, Jan. 14, 1804. Baptized by Brother Paul Weiss. Married Miss Wade, of New York. He had one son. In 1833, July 30, married Catharine Leibert, of Emmaus. Of the four children of this marriage, three survived. A railroad accident caused his death.

538. **Francis Henry Wenhold.** xvii, s. 12. Sept. 4. Infant son of Charles and Araminta (Brunner) Wenhold.

539. **Jacobina Fredericka Miller.** vii, n. 17. Oct. 27. Born at Nazareth, Sept. 29, 1772. Married Henry Christian Miller, Dec. 13, 1795, who died Sept. 17, 1833.

540. **David Theodore Riegel.** xvii, s. 13. Nov. 11. Infant son of Daniel and Hannah (Weber) Riegel.

1842.

541. **Augustus Alexander Albright.** xvii, s. 14. Jan. 14. Son of Henry and Catharine Louisa Albright. Born March 11, 1834.

542. **Maria Magdalena Hessler,** m.n. Koehler. vi, n. 17. Feb. 14. Born in Maguntschi, Sept. 21, 1751. In 1765 to Bethlehem, then to Heidelberg, Lititz, and Lebanon, where she nursed her aged father until 1794, when she married William Hessler, of Hope, N.J., where she lived till 1808. Then moved to Nazareth. Her husband died Dec. 22, 1834.

543. **Wilhelmina Adelaide Schaefer,** m. n. Giersch. xii, n. 18. Feb. 19. Daughter of Christian F. and Elizabeth Giersch. Born Dec. 11, 1812, in Plainfield. Married May 19, 1833, to Solomon Schaefer. She had four children.

544. **Maria Salome Clewell.** x, n. 13. March 2. Unmarried sister. Daughter of George and Anna Maria Clewell. Born in Plainfield, May 3, 1767. Confirmed in Schoeneck, 1780. In 1809 moved into the Sisters' House.

545. **Elizabeth Michael,** m.n. Giersch. xi, n. 18. March 13. Born in Bethlehem, March 26, 1773. Married Christian Samuel Michael, March 2, 1800. She had two sons and two daughters. Her husband died March 1, 1835.

546. **Jacob Samuel Kram.** xvii, s. 15. April 9. Infant son of John and Rebecca Kram.

547. **Oliver Benjamin Albright.** xvii, s. 16. April 24. Son of Henry and Catharine Louisa (Clewell) Albright. Aged ten years.

548. **Anna Maria Schleppe.** v, n. 17. May 21. Infant daughter of Abraham and Elizabeth (Giersch) Schleppe.

549. **Anna Rosina Wolle.** v, n. 18. May 24. Infant daughter of Edwin P. and Sarah Louisa (Kummer) Wolle.

550. **Martin Klose.** xvii, s. 17. July 21. Pupil in Nazareth Hall. Born June 29, 1833, in Sharon, Barbadoes, W. I., where his parents were missionaries.

551. **Anna Johanna Clewell,** m.n. Knauss. ix, n. 18. Aug. 1. Born in Emmaus, March 31, 1765. Married in Schoeneck, April 13, 1788, George Clewell. Her husband died March 17, 1816. Moved to Nazareth in 1825. She had four sons and three daughters, two sons dying before their mother.

552. **Beatus Riegel.** xvii, s. 18. Sept. 30. Infant son of Daniel and Hannah Riegel.

553. **Joseph Schweisshaupt.** xviii, s. 7. Dec. 8. Born May 30, 1764, on the road to Lititz, when his parents were fleeing from pursuing Indians. In his childhood he was in the Nazareth nursery. Married Rosina Busch, of Lititz, June 5, 1797. Of his four children, only one daughter survived. He served as organist and musical director, and as a member of the "Aufseher Collegium," or Trustees of the Church.

1843.

554. **Rosina Schweisshaupt,** m.n. Busch. viii, n. 18. Jan. 12. Daughter of John and Maria Busch, and widow of Joseph Schweisshaupt. Born in the neighborhood of York, Pa., May 4, 1768. In 1782 entered the Sisters' House at Lititz. United with the congregation in 1783.

555. **Christian Henry Beck.** xviii, s. 8. Feb. 21. Born in Bethlehem, July 17, 1757. When one and one-half years old, was placed in the Nazareth nursery at Ephrata; later attended the school in the Hall. United with the congregation in 1776. Married Anna Christiana Eyerly, Sept. 26, 1790. Seven children; two sons and five daughters, one son and a daughter preceding him into eternity. In 1800 built a house and brewery near Nazareth and carried on beer brewing and butchering. For twenty years he was a member of the "Aufseher Collegium." His wife died Nov. 21, 1833.

556. **Emma Cornelia Florenschuetz.** iv, n. 18. May 14. A child.

557. **Johanna Sophia Hoeber,** m.n. Lehman. vii, n. 18. May 29. Widow of Rev. Nicholas Hoeber, a minister of the Church. Born April 18, 1761, in Neukirchen, in Upper Lusatia. Confirmed by Carl Rudolph Reichel. When 25 years old, united with the Herrnhut congregation. After living eight years in Neusalz, went to America, with Brother and Sister John Gebhard Cunow, in whose family she lived until her marriage to Nicholas Hoeber, Feb. 14, 1799. She had two sons. Served in several congregations, with her husband, who died Aug. 4, 1830. She was laboress among the widows for some years.

558. **Peter Titus.** (Colored.) xviii, s. 9. Aug. 12. Born in New York, March 28, 1770. Being a slave he was brought to Bethlehem by his owner, Christian Froehlich, where he was baptized March 23, 1785. Married Mary

Boston, a colored sister of Christianspring, and worked on the farm at Gnadenthal for many years. Then moved into the Ephrata building, performing day-laborer's work, assisting, in various ways at the Hall, pulling the bellows in the church, etc. He died in the Alms House.

559. **Francisca Louisa Grunewald.** iii, n. 18. Sept. 9. Infant daughter of Theodore Ferdinand and Amelia Eliza (Bardill) Grunewald.

560. **Adeline Olivia Beck.** xv, n. 1. Sept. 9. Infant daughter of Jacob Ferdinand and Caroline Lisetta (Stauber) Beck.

561. **Lewis Ferdinand Lambert.** xviii, s. 10. Oct. 25. Born in Soldin, Prussia, March 6, 1781. Learned the weaver's trade. Served for a number of years in the Prussian army. Became acquainted with the Brethren in 1804. After having lived in various German congregations, he was received into the congregation at Gnadau. From 1810-15 he was assistant in some of the schools, and Diaspora laborer in Brunswick. Two years later he was called to Herrnhut, and then to Ebersdorf, finally to America, landing in Baltimore in 1822. Soon after he was called to Schoeneck, as pastor, and married Anna Charlotte Bechler, July 8, 1822. He had eight children; five sons and three daughters, of whom the daughters and two sons died. After thirteen years of service in Schoeneck, he was called to Hebron, Lebanon Co., Pa. After living a short time in Bethlehem and Nazareth, he was appointed to Hopedale, Pa., Oct., 1838. He had been ordained, Aug. 4, 1822, as Deacon by Bishop C. G. Hueffel. In 1842 retired to Nazareth.

562. **Clara Amelia Hagen.** xv, n. 2. Nov. 16. Infant daughter of Rev. Francis F. and Clara (Reichel) Hagen.

563. **Beata Riegel.** xv, n. 3. Nov. 20. Infant daughter of Daniel and Hannah Riegel.

1844.

564. **Anna Maria Bauer,** m.n. Romig. vi, n. 18. Feb. 11. Born March 7, 1763, in Allemängel. In 1770 moved, with her parents, to Emmaus. There she married Gottlieb Bauer. She had ten children, of whom one daughter died. In 1800 moved to Bushkill township. Her husband died June 22, 1811. In 1833 moved to Nazareth.

565. **Frederick Wolle.** xviii, s. 11. March 7. Son of J. Frederick and Sabina (Henry) Wolle. Born in Bushkill Township, Sept. 21, 1814. In 1821 moved to Nazareth; then to Bethlehem, where he was confirmed. Moved to New York in 1836, carrying on the tinsmith business there. The same year married Caroline Lucinda Helwig. In 1840 moved to Nazareth. He had three daughters and a son.

566. **Maria Bauer,** m.n. Cassler. xvi, n. 1. June 10. Born Dec. 9, 1803, in Plainfield Township. Married Charles Lewis Bauer, Sept. 22, 1833, and then united with the Brethren's Church, having previously belonged to the Lutheran. She had five children.

567. **Sarah Emma Cassler.** xv, n. 4. July 4. Infant daughter of Joseph and Savannah Cassler.

568. **Peter Penn Walter.** xix, s. 18. Oct. 25. Infant son of Dr. Philip and Rachel B. (Sellers) Walter.

1845.

569. **Henry Albright.** xviii, s. 12. Jan. 27. Born Aug. 5, 1772, in Lititz. Lived
in Nazareth since 1816, after having resided in Lititz, Gnadenhütten, Ohio,
Shippensburg, and a number of other places. Married Anna Barbara
Hubley, March 27, 1794, with whom he had ten children, and who died
Feb. 25, 1830. Married Catharine Louisa Beck, m.n. Clewell, with whom
he had four children.

570. **Ellen Hortensia Schaefer.** xv, n. 5. April 13. Infant daughter of Solomon
Schaefer.

571. **Caroline Sophia Clewell.** ii, n. 18. May 28. Daughter of Jacob and Anna
Rebecca (Seyfried) Clewell. Aged 12 years.

572. **William Cornelius Kluge.** xix, s. 17. June 27. Pupil in Nazareth Hall.
Son of Rev. John Peter and Maria Eliza (Albright) Kluge. Born Oct.
16, 1835.

573. **Susan L. Peck.** xv, n. 6. July 12. Daughter of David L. and Margaret
Peck. Aged five years.

574. **Eugene Alexander Clewell.** xix, s. 16. July 14. Infant son of Jacob and
Anna Rebecca (Seyfried) Clewell.

575. **Beatus Riegel.** xix, s. 15. Aug. 5. Infant son of Daniel and Hannah
Riegel.

576. **John Bardill.** xviii, s. 13. Oct. 1. Born Nov. 17, 1757, in Graubundten.
Served, for some time, as soldier. Received into the the congregation at
Neuwied, 1777. 1778-86 lived in Gnadau. In 1786 he was called to mission
service in Antigua, W. I. Married Anna Barbara Mettler, Aug. 19, 1787.
He had two children; a son and a daughter. In 1799, on account of the
impaired health of his wife, came to Pennsylvania. Served as minister in
New York and at Emmaus, from 1801-07 ; when he retired to Nazareth,
serving later, for a short time, as missionary among the Indians at Goshen,
Ohio. His wife died in 1831.

577. **Peter Stoudt** (Stout.) xviii, s. 14. Oct. 7. Born in Saucon Township, Oct. 24,
1782. United with the congregation in Bethlehem in 1805. Moved to
Nazareth and married Anna Rebecca Miksch, Sept. 23, 1810. He had seven
children. For many years was the grave digger. Died of small-pox.

578. **Sybilla Brunner,** m.n. Weinland. xvi, n. 2. Oct. 7. Born Sept. 10. 1781,
at Trapp. Moved to Hope, N. J., and later to Bethlehem. Married Christian
Brunner, Feb. 9, 1804. Had three children ; a son and two daughters.

1846.

579. **Lewis Charles Beitel.** xix, s. 14. Jan. 2. Infant son of William and Eliza
Ann (Ruch) Beitel.

580. **Beatus de Schweinitz.** xix, s. 13. Jan. 20. Infant son of Rev. Emil A. and
Sophia A. (Herman) de Schweinitz.

581. **Anna Christina Hillman,** m.n. Beck. xvi, n. 3. Feb. 25. Born in Christiansspring, Dec. 30, 1798. Married Joseph Henry Hillman, May 25, 1823. She
had eight children ; five sons and three daughters.

582. **Philip Hasselberger.** xviii, s. 15. May 3. Born Nov. 8, 1800, in Hesse
Darmstadt. Married Lydia Bauer.

583. **Julianna Clewell.** x, n. 14. May 16. Unmarried sister; daughter of Franz Clewell. Born March 16, 1768, in Bushkill Township. In 1781 united with the congregation in Schoeneck. In her thirteenth year she lost her right hand, in an accident at a cider-mill. In 1798 moved to Nazareth, with her mother, whom she nursed until her death. Then moved into the Sisters' House. In 1831 she broke her left hand. She was a friend of little children. In 1844 she suffered from an apoplectic stroke, and Brother and Sister Francis Miksch took charge of her, nursing her faithfully until her death.

584. **Gideon Andrew Cassler.** xix, s. 12. June 28. Infant son of Joseph and S. (Frey) Cassler.

585. **Samuel Frederick Reinke.** xix, s. 11. Aug. 16. Son of Rev. Samuel and Charlotte Sophia (Hueffel) Reinke. Born in Lancaster, Pa., Oct. 14, 1836. Died only thirteen days after entering Nazareth Hall as a pupil.

586. **Julianna Miksch,** m.n. Leinbach. xvi, n. 4. Sept. 18. Born June 19, 1789, in Graceham, Md. Daughter of Christian and Rosina Leinbach. In 1803 entered the school at Lititz, and two years later united with the congregation. Married Nathaniel Miksch, Nov. 17, 1811. She had nine children; seven sons and two daughters, of whom two sons preceded her into eternity.

1847.

587. **Beata Musselman.** xv, n. 7. Feb. 18. Infant daughter of Christian and Sarah (Zimmerman) Musselman.

588. **Maria Rosina Clewell,** m.n. Kreiter. xvi, n 5. April 17. Born May 3, 1776, in Lancaster. Her parents were Mennonites. Baptized in Lititz in her twelfth year. She lived in the Sisters' House. In 1798 moved to Nazareth, and married Christian Clewell. She had six children; five sons and a daughter.

589. **Emmanuel Rondthaler.** xx, s. 1. June 6. Presbyter. Born July 27, 1764, in Zirwenz, near Lauenburg, Prussia, where his father was a Lutheran minister. Confirmed in the Lutheran Church. In 1788 united with the Brethren's congregation in Neusalz. In 1791 he was called to Herrnhut, where he served in various capacities. 1795-1805 Brethren's laborer in Sarepta, Russia. In 1806 came to this country. Pastor at York, Pa. 1819 to 1839 pastor in Nazareth, and member of the Provincial Board. His first wife was Catharine Wuensch, with whom he had one daughter. She died in 1808. His second wife was Maria Christina Toon. She had five sons and two daughters. One son died in childhood. Three sons, Ambrose, Emanuel and Edward, entered the ministry.

590. **Ellen Rebecca Seyfried.** xv, n. 8. June 9. Infant daughter of Christian Seyfried.

591. **Henry David Michael.** xix, s. 10. June 26. Infant son of David Michael.

592. **Christian Clewell.** xviii, s. 16. Aug. 14. Born, Nov. 2, 1770, near Schoeneck. In 1798, after his marriage, moved to Niesky.

593. **Christian Henry Beitel.** xx, s. 2. Sept. 16. Born in Bethlehem, Sept. 22, 1788. Moved, with his parents, to Christianspring. In 1808 united with the congregation. Married Rosina Miksch, April 4, 1811. He lived for thirty years on one of the Nazareth farms. Later on one of his own. He had four daughters.

594. **Elizabeth Ehrenhard, m.n.** Arnold. xvi, n. 6. Sept. 24. Born in Upper Milford Township, Oct. 26, 1788. United with the Emmaus congregation. Married Jacob Ehrenhard in 1821, who died in 1825. Since 1837 lived with her daughter, Mrs. Kichline, near Nazareth.

595. **William Cullen Walter.** xviii, s. 17. Oct. 30. Son of Dr. Philip and Rachel B. (Sellers) Walter. Born July 24, 1829. He had but recently begun the study of medicine, when, by accident, he was fatally shot.

596. **Benezet Edwin Wolle.** xix, s. 9. Nov. 24. Son of Edwin P. and Louisa (Kummer) Wolle.

597. **Amy Amanda Riegel.** xv, n. 9. Dec. 9. Infant daughter of Daniel and Hannah Riegel.

1848.

598. **Beatus Musselman.** xix, s. 8. March 1. Infant son of Christian and Sarah (Zimmerman) Musselman.

599. **Theodore Ferdinand Grunewald.** xx, s. 3. Aug. 9. Born April 24, 1809, in Gnadau. He came to America in 1833. Married Amelia Eliza Bardill, Oct. 6, 1836. He had two children, a son and a daughter, the latter dying in childhood.

600. **Otto Bibinger.** xix, s. 7. Sept. 10. A child.

601. **Elizabeth Bibinger.** xv, n. 10. Sept. 15. Twin sister of the last named.

602. **Anna Cornelia Schaefer.** xv, n. 11. Dec. 5. Infant daughter of Solomon and Anna (Luckenbach) Schaefer.

1849.

603. **Anna Walker.** x, n. 15. Jan. 4. Unmarried sister. Born in 1764 or 65. During the flight of the people from Wyoming, on account of Indian troubles, she came to Hope, N. J., with her parents. Having been taken ill, her parents left her at the home of Brother Hauser. In 1785 she came to Nazareth, and lived sixty-three years in the Sisters' House. " Die letzte aus der alten Zeit."

604. **Lucinda Emilie Beck.** x, n. 16. April 8. Aged twenty-nine years.

605. **Anna Magdalene Beitel, m.n.** Romig. xvi, n. 7. Aug. 9. Born near Emmaus, Feb. 22, 1792. Moved with her widowed mother to Emmaus, when eight years of age, and united with the congregation in 1806. Married John Beitel, April 23, 1810. She had three sons and three daughters.

1850.

606. **Sandford Frederick Neumeyer.** xix, s. 6. April 15. Infant son of John and Caroline (Schultz) Neumeyer.

607. **Mary Louisa Beitel.** xvi, n. 8. May 22. Daughter of John and Anna M. (Romig) Beitel. Aged 14 years.

608. **Caroline Lisetta Beck, m.n.** Stauber. xvi, n. 9. Oct. 16. Born at Schoeneck, March 15, 1802. In 1820 moved to the Sisters' House in Nazareth. Married Jacob Ferdinand Beck, Jan. 14, 1827. She had eleven children ; three sons and eight daughters ; one son and a daughter died before their mother.

1851.

609. **Rosina Beitel, m.n. Miksch.** xvi, n. 10. April 17. Born in Christianspring, Aug. 2, 1791. Her mother died in 1806, and she kept house for her father until his marriage to Maria Cath. Hoeck. Married Christian Henry Beitel, April 4, 1811. Her husband died Sept. 16, 1847. She had four daughters.

610. **Henry Abraham Christ.** xix, s. 5. Aug. 10. Son of Richard Benj. and Fredericka (Danke) Christ.

611. **Sarah Julia Weber.** xv, n. 12. Infant daughter of George and Maria M. Weber.

612. **John Horton Miksch.** xix, s. 4. Sept. 3. Infant son of Joseph and Lucinda (Riegel) Miksch.

613. **Henrietta Matilda Bute.** xvi, n. 11. Sept. 10. Daughter of Dr. George H. and Mary (Bardill) Bute. Born in Paramaribo, S. A., July 5, 1830, where her parents were missionaries. Came to Nazareth, in her childhood, with her parents. Later, lived in Philadelphia. She was a teacher in the Girls' School at Nazareth.

614. **Georgianna Augusta Bute.** xvi, n. 12. Nov. 7. Daughter of Dr. Geo. H. and Mary (Bardill) Bute. Born in Philadelphia, Aug. 1, 1836.

615. **Johannes Maehr.** xx, s. 4. Dec. 11. Missionary. Born Nov. 8, 1764, in Prussia. Came to Neusalz, 1789, then to Niesky, Herrnhut and Neudietendorf. United with the Brethren's Church in 1789. In 1794 was called to Bambey, Surinam, as missionary. In 1795 he was very sick with yellow fever, and, as he appeared to have died, was already prepared for burial. In 1800, Aug. 4, married the widow Metz, m.n. Tshudy, in Paramaribo. In 1813 left Bambey, and the mission was abandoned, after he had been there more than eighteen years and his wife upwards of twelve. He continued several years in Paramaribo, then being called to Bethany, St. Jan, W. I. In 1818 to Friedensthal, St. Croix; in 1819 to Bethany. In 1819 he came to America on furlough, on account of impaired health. His wife died at Lititz, May 21, 1821. Having received a call to the West Indies, he married Elizabeth Fahs, Sept. 2, 1821. In 1822 arrived in St. Thomas; later served in New Herrnhut, Friedensberg, St. Croix. In 1824 returned to America on account of failing health.

1852.

616. **Caroline Dorothea Michael.** xvi, n. 13. Jan. 6. Unmarried sister. Born Feb. 7, 1802, in Nazareth.

617. **Eugene Nathaniel Miksch.** xix, s. 3. Jan. 13. Infant son of Richard and Cecilia Henrietta (Clewell) Miksch.

618. **Lewis Richard Seyfried.** xix, s. 2. Feb. 14. Infant son of Joseph and Antoinette (Miksch) Seyfried.

619. **Sarah Jane Silver.** xv, n. 13. April 5. Infant daughter of John and Marietta (Wright) Silver.

620. **Andrew Whitesell.** xx, s. 5. April 17. Son of Richard and Elizabeth Whitesell. Born Jan. 13, 1779, near Hope, N.J. In 1792 came to Nazareth, to learn gunsmith trade. In 1801, Jan. 26, married Elizabeth Weinland, daughter of John and Phoebe Weinland. She had nine children, five sons and four daughters. In 1805 moved to Friedensthal; 1807 to Mt. Bethel, where his wife died in 1816. In 1817 married Elizabeth Clewell, daughter

of John and Hannah Clewell. In 1818 moved to Nazareth, where he was confirmed in 1819. He had two daughters by his second marriage. In 1838 his wife died.

621. **Thomas William Beitel.** xviii, s. 18. June 10. Son of William and Eliza (Ruch) Beitel. Born Sept. 26, 1838.

622. **Anna Maria Seyfried.** xv, n. 14. June 29. Daughter of Joseph and Antoinette (Miksch) Seyfried. Aged three years.

623. **Henry Christian Beitel Shireman.** xix, s. 1. July 31. Born Aug. 30, 1848.

624. **Laura Virginia Daniel.** xv, n. 15. Aug. 9. A child.

625. **Maria Louisa Hark.** xvii, n. 1. Aug. 9. Infant daughter of Dr. Joseph and Louisa (Bute) Hark.

626. **Jacob Daniel Spengler.** xxi, s. 1. Aug. 27. Infant son of David and Helena (Siegfried) Spengler.

627. **William Christ Albright.** xxi, s. 2. Sept. 2. Infant son of Lafayette and Amelia (Christ) Albright, of Lewisburgh, Pa. Died while parents were here on a visit.

628. **Antoinette Clarissa Seyfried,** m.n. Miksch. xvi, n. 14. Sept. 3. Born May 19, 1817, in Nazareth. Married Joseph Seyfried, Oct. 17, 1839. She had six children, four sons and two daughters, of whom two sons and a daughter died in childhood.

629. **Frank Senseman.** xxi, s. 3. Sept. 10. Son of Comenius and Sophia Henrietta (Reichel) Senseman.

630. **Henry David Schaefer.** xxi, s. 4. Dec. 29. Son of Solomon and Anna (Luckenbach) Schaefer.

1853.

631. **John Ehrhardt.** xxi, s. 5. Jan. 21. Infant son of Frederick and Mary Ehrhardt.

632. **Louisa Henrietta Hay,** m.n. Stotz. xvi, n. 15. Feb. 22. Daughter of Joseph and Henrietta (Ernst) Stotz. Married Jefferson Hay, Nov. 17, 1849. She had a son and a daughter. Aged 24 years.

633. **Mary Catharine Best.** xv, n. 16. March 16. Infant daughter of Peter and Ellen (Mutchler) Best.

634. **Antoinette Sophia Michael.** xvi, n. 16. April 7. Daughter of Gotthold and Elizabeth Michael. Born May 17, 1837.

635. **John Lewis Schmidt.** xx, s. 6. May 28. Born March 25, 1783, in Canton Wafdt, Switzerland. Confirmed in the Reformed Church. Married Magdalena Siegenthaler, June 15, 1807. He had five children, of whom two survived. In 1825 came to America. Lived in Moore township, then Filetown, and united with Schoeneck congregation. Moved to Nazareth in 1851.

636. **Joseph Abraham Hay.** xxi, s. 6. July 11. Infant son of Jefferson and Louisa Henrietta (Stotz) Hay.

637. **Anna Lucia Hillman.** xv, n. 17. July 12. Infant daughter of Owen and Matilda (Riegel) Hillman.

638. **Cornelius Immanuel Brunner.** xxi, s. 7. July 18. Infant son of Henry Jacob and Henrietta Louisa (Beck) Brunner.

639. **Mary Jane Hay.** xv, n. 18. July 19. Daughter of Jefferson and Louisa Henrietta (Stotz) Hay. (An epidemic of dysentery prevailed and many children died.)

5

640. **Cecilia Louisa Brunner.** xvii, n. 2. July 22. Daughter of Henry Jacob and Henrietta (Beck) Brunner.
641. **Caroline Angelica Belling.** xvii, n. 3. Aug. 8. Infant daughter of Sylvester and Seraphina (Wilhelm) Belling.
642. **Edmund Emilius Clewell.** xxi, s. 8. Aug. 9. Infant son of Thomas and Florentine (Leibert) Clewell.
643. **Eugene Henry Michael.** xxi, s. 9. Aug. 14. Infant son of James and Mary Ann (Engler) Michael.
644. **George Ziegler.** xxi, s. 10. Aug. 14. Infant son of George and Johannette (Kann) Ziegler.
645. **Irene Maria Wolle.** xvii, n. 4. Aug. 20. Infant daughter of Edwin P. and Louisa (Kummer) Wolle.
646. **Maurice Winfield Milchsack.** xxi, s. 11. Aug. 22. Infant son of Henry and Ellen (Beitel) Milchsack.
647. **Mary Ann Miller.** xvi, n. 17. Sept. 5. Unmarried sister. Born Sept. 11, 1817, in Lower Saucon. When three years old, her uncle and aunt, Brother and Sister David Warner, took charge of her, living at that time in Quakertown. In 1827 moved to Bethlehem, where she was confirmed. In consequence of a fever in 1830, she became lame.
648. **Valeria Jane Best.** xvii, n. 5. Sept. 9. Daughter of Peter and Ellen (Mutchler) Best.
649. **Susan Danke.** m.n. Ehrenhard. xvi, n. 18. Dec. 27. Daughter of Jacob and Susan Ehrenhard; born in Emmaus, Dec. 25, 1797. Married Franz Chr. Danke, May 26, 1819. She had one daughter, who married Richard Christ.

1854.

650. **Franz Christian Danke.** xx, s. 7. Jan. 26. Born June 20, 1785, in Nazareth. In 1811 married Anna Maria Ehrenhard, of Emmaus, who died May 9, 1818. Married Susan Ehrenhard, of Emmaus, May 26, 1819. One daughter. His wife had died only a month before him. Besides following his trade, he also had charge of the large granaries of the congregation to the rear of the Hall. He was a faithful and respected man.
651. **Maria Christina Rondthaler,** m.n. Toon. xx, n. 1. Jan. 29. Born near Emmaus, June 12, 1784. Confirmed in Bethlehem, in 1801. Married the widower, the Rev. Emmanuel Rondthaler, July 14, 1808. She had seven children, (two of whom died) and served, with her husband, in York, Pa., and in Nazareth twenty years. Her husband died June 6, 1847.
652. **Johann Traugott Gerlach.** xx, s. 8. Feb. 18. Son of Daniel and Anna Maria (Lang) Gerlach. Born Aug. 9, 1773, near Görlitz, Upper Lusatia. United with the congregation in Niesky, Aug. 13, 1787. Came to America in 1803. Lived in the Brethren's House in Lititz. He was a dyer and stocking weaver by trade. In 1812 came to the Brethren's House in Nazareth. Married Sarah Diely in 1814. By this marriage he had a daughter. His wife died in 1815, Dec. 15. In June, 1816, married Elizabeth Seyfried in Lititz. He had a son and a daughter by this marriage. He died very suddenly, aged 80 years.
653. **Mary Elizabeth Gerlach,** m.n. Seyfried. xx, n. 2. April 13. Born in Plainfield Township, Feb. 27, 1789. She lived in the Sisters' House in

1812. In 1814 to Lititz. Married John Traugott Gerlach in June, 1816. Her husband had died in February.

654. **Joseph Henry Hillman.** xx, s. 9. July 20. Born March 30, 1801, in Bethlehem. Confirmed in Nazareth in 1824. Married Anna Christine Beck, May 25, 1823. He had five sons and two daughters, of whom two sons died before their father. His wife died Feb. 25, 1846. Married Mary Crawford, m.n. Spangenberg. In 1847 he was Sheriff of Northampton County.

655. **Herman Kampman Van Vleck.** xxi, s. 12. July 22. Infant son of Henry J. and Augusta (Beear) Van Vleck.

656. **Elizabeth Maehr,** m.n. Fahs. xx, n. 3. Sept. 9. Born May 9, 1775, in Heidelberg Township, Pa. In her eleventh year moved to York, where she was confirmed in 1793. In 1801 moved to the Sisters' House in Lititz, where she lived twenty years, and was sick-nurse during a portion of the time. Married John Maehr, Sept. 2, 1821, and went with him, as missionary, to St. Thomas, W.I. After three years, on account of failing health, returned to the United States, and lived in Nazareth. Her husband died, Dec., 1851.

657. **Caroline Elizabeth Kichline.** xvii, n. 6. Oct. 20. Daughter of Conrad and Eloisa Kichline.

658. **Laura Emmaline Flammer.** xvii, n. 7. Oct. 30. Infant daughter of Emanuel and Henrietta (Venter) Flammer.

1855.

659. **Mary Clewell,** m.n. Christ. xx, n. 4. Feb. 12. Born Dec. 31, 1780, in Nazareth. Married John Clewell, Jan. 28, 1806, and moved to Bushkill; in 1819 to a farm at Schoeneck. Husband died 1845, and she moved to Nazareth some time after. She had seven children, of whom four died before their mother.

660. **Hannah Riegel,** m.n. Weber. xx, n. 5. Feb. 23. Born in Allen Township, Aug. 27, 1802. In 1828 married Daniel Riegel. In 1851 united with the Moravian Church. She had fourteen children, of whom six died in childhood.

661. **Beatus Huebinger.** xxi, s. 13. March 6. Son of Frederick and Louisa (Hoeber) Huebinger.

662. **Ellen Bertha Lorenz.** xvii, n. 8. Oct. 14.

1856.

663. **Anna Catharine Hoeck.** xx, n. 6. April 15. Daughter of George and Maria Catharine (Wingas) Hoeck. Born near Elberfeld, Westphalia. On the journey to America in 1795 her father died. Having lost all her possessions, her mother arrived in this country, with only one of her five children, the others having died. She and her daughter found a home in Gnadenthal. Received into the congregation in 1802. For many years she was cook in the Sisters' House. In 1823 became assistant to the Warden of the Sisters' House. In 1850 moved into the home of Brother and Sister Leibfried. Aged 68 years.

664. **John Jacob Schmidt.** xx, s. 10. May 27. Son of John Lewis and Magdalena Schmidt. Born in 1812, Oct. 25, near Berne, Switzerland. In 1825 came to this country with his parents. In 1828 confirmed in the Reformed Church by the Rev. Mr. Pomp.

665. **Beata Moser.** xvii, n. 9. July 29. Infant daughter of Stephen and Maria (Beck) Moser.

666. **Maria Caroline Lennert,** m. n. Schmidt. xx, n. 7. Nov. 5. Daughter of Dr. Henry B. Schmidt. Born Aug. 16, 1812, in Nazareth. In 1827 attended the Ladies' Seminary in Bethlehem, and was there confirmed in 1828. Served as teacher, several years, in the Nazareth congregation school. Married the Rev. William L. Lennert, Dec. 6, 1836, and served with him ten years at York, Pa. In 1847 at Lebanon, and in Nazareth seven years. She had four sons, two of whom died before their mother.

667. **Robert Henry Lennert.** xxi, s. 14. Dec. 30. Infant son of William L. and Caroline Lennert.

1857.

668. **Jacob Ferdinand Beck.** xx, s. 11. March 26. Son of Christian Henry and Anna Christina (Eyerly) Beck. Born in Christianspring, Aug. 20, 1791. Married Anna Rosina Levering, Feb. 18, 1816. She had five daughters. His wife died June 3, 1825. Married Caroline Lisetta Stauber, January 14, 1827. She had three sons and eight daughters. Wife died Oct. 16, 1850. Married Dorothea (Friebele) Hessler, March 26, 1856. Died suddenly, in the Post Office in Wm. Beitel's store.

669. **Anna Elizabeth Senseman,** m.n. Ritter. xx, n. 8. April 18. Born in Philadelphia, Sept. 7, 1779. Married Christian D. Senseman, Nov. 27, 1806. In 1807 united with the congregation. She had five sons and two daughters, the latter deceased. Her husband died December 13, 1834. Since 1852 she was totally blind.

670. **Eloisa Kichline,** m.n. Sachsen. xviii, n. 1. April 18. Born Nov. 19, 1811, in Upper Saucon. Confirmed in Emmaus, 1826. Married Conrad Kichline, Sept. 14, 1836. Lived near Nazareth, and since 1855 in Nazareth. She had three daughters and a son, of whom a son and a daughter deceased.

671. **Christian Renatus Clewell.** xx, s. 12. April 25. Son of Christian and Maria Rosina (Kreiter) Clewell. Born Oct. 13, 1813, in Niesky. Confirmed 1829. Married Mary Ann Seiss, Oct. 31, 1837. He had three sons and a daughter, of whom one son died. His parents died in 1847. He was an excellent musician, performing on various instruments. In 1851 he abandoned his work and went to Philadelphia as teacher of music and organist. Died suddenly while playing the piano at a friend's house.

672. **Amelia Cornelia Engleman,** m.n. Rondthaler. xx, n. 9. July 14. Daughter of Emanuel and Maria Christina Rondthaler. Born in Nazareth, Dec. 11, 1824. Educated here and in Bethlehem Seminary. Confirmed, 1840. In 1849 teacher in Lititz. Married Charles Engleman, in Philadelphia, July, 1850. She had a daughter and two sons, of whom one of the latter died. Her remains were brought here for interment.

673. **Lewis David Lambert.** xx, s. 13. Aug. 15. Son of Lewis Ferdinand and Charlotte (Bechler) Lambert. Born in Hebron, Pa., Feb. 14, 1836. Educated at Nazareth Hall. In 1856 taught school in Hazleton, Pa.; later in Schuylkill Haven. Went to Philadelphia, in order to enter business; taken ill with varioloid, and died there. Remains were brought here for interment.

674. **Mary Lauretta Beitel.** xvii, n. 10. Aug. 19. Daughter of William and Eliza (Ruch) Beitel. Born Dec. 5, 1854.

675. **Ella Virginia Michael.** xvii, n. 11. Aug. 23. Infant daughter of James and Margaret Michael.

676. **Mary Alice Weaver.** xx, n. 10. Aug. 23. Daughter of Jacob and Margaret Weaver. Born in Forks Township, Jan. 12, 1845.

677. **Beatus Flammer.** xxi, s. 15. Sept. 29. Infant son of John and Henrietta Flammer.

678. **Gustav Adolph Lorenz.** xxi, s. 16. Oct. 2. A small child.

679. **Caroline Kuest.** xvii, n. 12. Oct. 7. Daughter of John George and Louisa (Zorn) Kuest. Born in Baden, Feb. 27, 1849. Came to America, with her parents, in 1852. Burned while making a fire, and died the following day.

680. **Mary Kimball,** m.n. Weinland. xviii, n. 2. Oct. 24. Daughter of John and Phoebe Weinland. Born in Philadelphia, March 6, 1780. Moved to Hope, N. J. There married. Since the death of her husband, she lived in Easton, where she died. Remains brought here for interment.

681. **Milton Henry Beck.** xxi, s. 17. Nov. 17. Infant son of Jacob and Lydia (Nolf) Beck.

1858.

682. **Maria Louisa Wilhelm,** m.n. Leibfried. xx, n. 11. March 13. Daughter of J. C. and Harriet (Beitel) Leibfried. Born July 7, 1836. Confirmed 1851. Married James H. Wilhelm, Oct. 12, 1854. She had one daughter.

683. **Emil William Lorenz.** xxi, s. 18. March 25. Small child.

684. **Adam Daniel.** xx, s. 14. April 12. (A member of the Reformed Church.) Born in Allen Township, Oct. 30, 1781. Married Catharine Wagener, of Easton, Dec., 1807. He had two sons and three daughters. His wife died May, 1850. During latter part of his life, had his home with his daughter, Mrs. William Christ.

685. **Anna Catharine Mueller.** xx, n. 12. April 25. Daughter of Abrm. and Maria S. Mueller. Born in Williams Township, July 29, 1801. Baptized and confirmed in the Reformed Church. Lived twenty years in Easton. Moved here, a few years ago, to her son, Wm. Ziegenfuss.

686. **John Henry Ziegenfuss.** xxii, s. 18. Aug. 7. Infant son of William and Rosina Barbara (Kunstman) Ziegenfuss.

687. **Clara Augusta Streepy.** xvii, n. 13. Aug. 21. Infant daughter of John and Seraphina (Statler) Streepy.

688. **Beatus Stoudt.** xxii, s. 17. Aug.

689. **Anna Johanna Arie.** xx, n. 13. Oct. 31. Daughter of Jacob and Marg. Arie (colored). Born in Christianspring, Nov. 9, 1781. United with the Schoeneck Church in 1794. Cook, etc., in the Sisters' House. In Nov., 1822, accompanied Brother and Sister Bechler to Lititz as child's-nurse. Returned to Nazareth Sisters' House. Aged 77 years.

690. **Lewis Alexander Clewell.** xx, s. 15. Dec. 3. Son of Sydney and Cecilia (Haman) Clewell. Born in Stockertown, Nov. 30, 1840. Died in Philadelphia, where his parents resided.

1859.

691. **Henry Gottfried Belling.** xx, s. 16. Jan. 13. Eldest son of John Fredr. and Anna Rosina Belling. Born in Nazareth, Sept. 16, 1783. Baptized by Brother Lembke. Confirmed 1811. Married Anna Catharine Brunner, April

19, 1807. During twenty-eight years lived near Schoeneck. In 1838 moved to the two-story log house (since torn down) near the Ephrata building. For many years suffered from occasional attacks of melancholy. On April 19, 1857, celebrated golden wedding. His married life was almost fifty-two years. He had six children; four sons and two daughters, of whom one son and two daughters preceded him into eternity.

692. **Charles Henry Shultz.** xxii, s. 16. Jan. 18. Son of Henry Shultz.

693. **Charles Lewis Meller.** xx, s. 17. Feb. 19. Born June 20, 1789, in Hope, N. J. When seven years old, moved, with his parents, to Graceham, Md., remaining there until his fifteenth year. After the death of his father, moved with his mother to Lititz, learning the trade of shoemaker in the Brethren's House. Confirmed in 1807. In 1814 moved to Nazareth. In 1817 married Anna Johanna Seyfried. Both in Lititz and Nazareth assisted with the church-music, until three years before his death. Paralysis occasioned lameness and affected his speech. He had six sons and three daughters. One son and a daughter preceded him into eternity.

694. **John Jacob Eckensberger.** xx, s. 18. March 13. Born Nov. 21, 1784, in Knittlingen, Würtemberg. Came to America in 1805, living in the Brethren's House. Received into the congregation in 1807. Married Maria Magd. Danke, Oct. 27, 1811. He had two sons and three daughters; a son and daughter died in their childhood. His wife died Oct. 12, 1816. Married Anna Johanna Clewell, April 7, 1817.

695. **Anna Elizabeth Ricksecker,** m. n. Beitel. xx, n. 14. April 4. Born in Nazareth, Dec. 21, 1789. Confirmed in 1803. Married John George Ricksecker, Nov. 11, 1810. She had three sons and two daughters, two sons and a daughter preceding her into eternity. Her husband died May 2, 1834. In 1842 she had an attack of melancholy, which continued nearly six years.

696. **George Rudolph Bardill.** xxiii, s. 1. May 16. Born Nov. 20, 1788, in St. John, Antigua, where his parents were missionaries. Confirmed in Nazareth in 1813. Married Catharine Elizabeth Schneider, Nov. 9, 1813. He had four children, two sons and two daughters, of whom the eldest son died in childhood. He had heart-trouble.

697. **Daniel Kingkinger** (Ginkinger.) xxiii, s. 2. June 7. Born in Plainfield Township, July 4, 1809. Baptized in the Lutheran Church. Married Rebecca Cassler, March, 1830. In 1840 he and his wife were confirmed at Schoeneck. In 1853 united with Church at Nazareth. He had eight children, three sons and five daughters, of whom two daughters died in childhood.

698. **Anna Rebecca Clewell,** m.n. Seyfried. xx, n. 15. June 15. Born in Bushkill Township, Nov. 22, 1798. Baptized and confirmed in Schoeneck. Married Jacob Clewell, Oct. 26, 1823. She had eight children. Two sons and two daughters survived their mother.

699. **Christian Henry Seyfried.** xxiii, s. 3. June 29. Son of John Seyfried. Born in Old Nazareth, Aug. 20, 1820. Confirmed in 1838. Married Anna Matilda Kram in March, 1844. He had six children, of whom one daughter died in childhood.

700. **Allen Eugene Snyder.** xxii, s. 15. Aug. 26. Infant son of Harrison and Angelica (Michael) Snyder.

701. **Henry Eugene Laubach.** xxii, s. 14. Sept. 19. Child.

702. **Johannes Gottlob Hark.** xxiii, s. 4. Sept. 20. Born in Barby, June 24, 1773. In his fifth year entered the school at Niesky. In 1786 returned to his home and learned the trade of bookbinder from his father. In 1808 moved with his father and two sisters to Niesky. Married Johanna Elizabeth Raschke, March 24, 1814. She died Sept. 2, 1849. In 1850, when seventy-seven years old, he came to this country, living with his son, Dr. Joseph Hark, at Nazareth. He had four children, two sons and two daughters.

1860.

703. **Lewis Frederick Clewell.** xxii, s. 13. Jan. 7. Infant son of Sylvester and Anna Maria (Bauer) Clewell.

704. **John Lewis Luckenbach.** xxiii, s. 5. April 27. Son of John Ludwig Luckenbach. Born in Long Swamp, Saucon Township, June 30, 1774. Moved, with his parents, to Hope, N. J., and was there baptized, as an adult, by Bishop Peter Boehler. He lived a number of years in Bethlehem, learning the trade of pumpmaking from Brother Bishop. Married Maria Kornman in 1799. Later, he moved to Easton, where he lived forty years. He served in the army in the war of 1812. His married life was nearly fifty-six years. A severe attack of paralysis deprived him of his speech, lamed him and affected his mind. He had six children, of whom a son and a daughter survived.

705. **George William Kram.** xxii, s. 12. Oct. 26. Son of Catharine Kram.

1861.

706. **Agnes Hortensia Miksch.** xvii, n. 14. Jan. 25. Infant daughter of Richard and Cecilia (Clewell) Miksch.

707. **Angelica Matilda Snyder,** m.n. Michael. xx, n. 16. Feb. 7. Daughter of Gotthold and Elizabeth Michael. Born April 27, 1840. Confirmed 1855. Married Harry Snyder, Oct. 15, 1857. She had one child, who died.

708. **Anna Maria Martin,** m.n. Alleman. xx, n. 17. Feb. 23. Born on Cherry Hill, Jan. 21, 1830. Confirmed in Schoeneck. Married C. Fredr. Martin, May 24, 1849.

709. **Andrew Gottfried Kern.** xxiii, s. 6. Jan. 26. Son of Andrew G. and Catharine Louisa (Levering) Kern. Born in Nazareth, May 19, 1822. Educated in Nazareth Hall and the Theological Seminary. During many years he was a teacher in Nazareth Hall. He was an excellent musician. Died in Lake City, Florida, where he was living, on account of his health. His remains were brought to Nazareth for interment, his funeral being held Feb. 26.

710. **Theresa Maria Caroline Ziegler.** xvii, n. 15. April 28. Infant daughter of George and Johannette (Kann) Ziegler.

711. **Anna Maria Bauer.** xx, n. 18. May 11. Born near Emmaus, Oct. 21, 1787. Her parents were Gottlieb and Anna M. Bauer. Lived, during many years, in the Sisters' House.

712. **Josephine Maria Smith.** xvii, n. 16. June 22. Infant daughter of the Rev. D. Z. Smith.

713. **Sarah Louisa Rothrock.** x, n. 17. July 17. Born in Springfield, Bucks Co., Pa., March 10, 1790. Baptized as an adult in Bethlehem in 1806. The first baptism in the new Moravian Church there. Came to Nazareth in 1812 and lived in the Sisters' House, where she served as sick-nurse for many years

714. **Daniel Wilhelm.** xxiii, s. 7. Aug. 3. Born Jan. 11, 1805, near Nazareth. His parents were John and Charlotte Wilhelm. Baptized by the Rev. Mr. Pomp, of Easton, and confirmed by him. His father died when he was only nine years old, and he then lived with his uncle, John Lawall. Married Maria Beck in 1826, and later moved to Nazareth. He was the head "diener" (sacristan) for many years.

715. **Francis Lewis Brunner.** xxii, s. 11. Aug. 26. Son of Henry J. and Henrietta Brunner.

716. **John Jacob Christ.** xxiii, s. 8. Nov. 3. Born June 3, 1781, in Nazareth, in the same house in which he died. Married Benigna Eliza Ebert, Nov. 25, 1805, who died the following year. In 1807, July 30, married Anna Justina Knauss of Bethlehem. Three children survived; two sons and a daughter.

1862.

717. **Anna Justina Christ,** m.n. Knauss. xviii, n. 3. Jan. 12. Born in Bethlehem, March 31, 1785. Married John Jacob Christ, in 1807. Her husband died Nov. 3, of the preceding year. She had four children, one of her sons dying in infancy.

718. **Emil Samuel Lambert.** xxiii, s. 9. Feb. 7. Son of the Rev. Lewis Ferdinand and Charlotte (Bechler) Lambert. Born June 7, 1826. Besides following a trade for some years, he taught in a public school, and, during the latter part of his life, was a physician. Since childhood he was lame.

719. **Almaretta Catharine Frankenfield.** xvii, n. 17. Feb. 7.

720. **Theodore Emanuel Etschman.** xxii, s. 10. April 3. Infant son of Francis and Fredericka Etschman. (The first funeral held in the new church.)

721. **Mary Christiana Brown.** xxi, n. 4. May 12. Daughter of Daniel and Lucinda (Ebbecke) Brown. Born Feb. 27, 1856.

722. **Florence Irene Ettwein.** xvii, n. 18. June 16. Infant daughter of Jacob and Sophia (Miksch) Ettwein.

723. **Benjamin Franklin Clewell.** xxii, s. 9. June 25. Son of Henry and Eliza (Peissert) Clewell. Born June 11, 1858.

724. **Franklin Levin Beck.** xxii, s. 8. July 7. Son of Jacob and Lydia (Nolf) Beck. Born May 2, 1861.

725. **Robert Edmund Ricksecker.** xxii, s. 7. July 15. Son of Edmund and Olivia (Miksch) Ricksecker. Born Oct. 1, 1855.

726. **Allen Jerome Beitel.** xxii, s. 6. Aug. 13. Son of Edward and Ebesina (Babp) Beitel. Born Jan. 9, 1861. (An epidemic of diphtheria caused the death of many children during the year.)

727. **Catharine Miksch,** m.n. Weinland. xviii, n. 4. Sept. 8. Born in Hope, N. J., Sept. 29, 1790. Married Jacob Miksch, Feb. 5, 1812. On Feb. 5, celebrated golden wedding. She had eight children, of whom two sons and a daughter preceded her into eternity.

728. **Lewis Christian Bachschmidt.** xxii, s. 5. Oct. 4. Son of Paul and Ida Bachschmidt. Born Jan. 8, 1854, in Camden Valley, N. Y.

729. **Benjamin Franklin Wolle.** xxii, s. 4. Oct. 8. Son of Edwin P. and Louisa (Kummer) Wolle. Born Nov. 29, 1853.

730. **Lucretia M. Hessler.** xviii, n. 5. Oct. 15. Daughter of Dorothea Hessler (Beck, m.n. Friebely.) Born in Schoeneck, March 26, 1841. In 1851 moved

with her parents to Hopedale; 1852 to Bethlehem; then to Plainfield, and finally to her uncle in Mauch Chunk.

731. **Robert Maurice Rauch.** xxii, s. 3. Oct. 16. Son of William F. and Emma (Peissert) Rauch.

732. **Samuel Augustus Schultz.** xxii, s. 2. Nov. 16. Son of Levi Schultz. Born March 16, 1858.

733. **Olivia Wilhelmina Huebinger.** xix, n. 1. Nov. 25. Daughter of Fredr. and Louisa (Hoeber) Huebinger. Born July 23, 1856.

734. **Adelaide Cornelia Schultz.** xix, n. 2. Dec. 22. Born Oct. 28, 1854.

1863.

735. **Anna Louisa Hartmann.** xix, n. 3. Jan. 14. Daughter of Frederick Hartmann. Born June 29, 1856.

736. **Joseph Oliver Schaefer.** xxiv, s. 1. Feb. 25. Son of Solomon Schaefer. Born May 19, 1841.

737. **Henry Augustus Van Vleck.** xxii, s. 1. April 10. Son of Henry J. and Augusta (Beear) Van Vleck. Born Sept. 30, 1852.

738. **Alice Elizabeth Herbst.** xix, n. 4. July 28. Daughter of William and Clementina (Ricksecker) Herbst.

739. **Anna Charlotte Lambert, m.n. Bechler.** xviii, n. 6. Sept. 15. Born on the Island of Oesel, Oct. 13, 1792. Teacher in Ebersdorf for a number of years. Married the Rev. Lewis Ferdinand Lambert, July 8, 1822, in this country. With him served at Schoeneck, Hebron and Hopedale. Her husband died Oct. 25, 1843. She had five sons and three daughters, all of whom preceded her into eternity.

740. **Cecilia Arabella Ricksecker.** xviii, n. 7. Sept. 28. Born June 25, 1821, in Schoeneck.

741. **Jacob Getz.** xxiii, s. 10. Oct. 11. Born in Burgberg, Germany, July 24, 1799. Lived in Stroudsburg; formerly in Nazareth, and belonged to this congregation.

742. **Gotthold Benjamin Michael.** xxiii, s. 11. Dec. 4. Son of David and Elizabeth (Giersch) Michael. Born in Nazareth, Oct. 30, 1807. Married in 1828. He had seven children, two of whom preceded him into eternity.

743. **Ferdinand Herbst.** xxiii, s. 12. Dec. 12. Born Nov. 28, 1832, near Christianspring. Married Harriet Clewell, May 23, 1854. He had three children.

744. **Elizabeth Schmick.** xviii, n. 8. Dec. 29. Born March 9, 1790, in Bethlehem. Moved to Nazareth in her childhood, with her parents. Lived several years in Ohio and Lititz. She was a teacher in the congregation school for girls during nine years.

1864.

745. **Maria Salome Brunner.** xviii, n. 9. Jan. 7. Born in Bethlehem, Sept. 29, 1790. When young, moved to Nazareth. Married John Jacob Brunner, Nov. 17, 1811. She had one son and three daughters. Her husband died Aug. 7, 1838.

746. **Emma Nitzsche, m.n. Venter.** xviii, n. 10. Feb. 23. Born in Philadelphia, June 16, 1838. When two years old, her parents moved to Nazareth. Married August Nitzsche, Jan. 11, 1862.

156

747. **Agnes Elizabeth Werner.** xix, n. 5. March 8. Daughter of William and Marietta Werner. Born July 9. 1862.

748. **Theophilus Wunderling.** xxiii, s. 13. April 8. Pastor at Nazareth. Born Sept. 10, 1824, in Gnadau, where his father, Christian Frederick Wunderling, was pastor. Studied in the Paedagogium in Niesky, and the Theological Seminary in Gnadenfeld. Teacher in Kleinwelka. In 1848 he was called to the United States, as teacher in Nazareth Hall. Received a call, as pastor, to Sharon, Ohio, Oct. 13, 1851, and married Cornelia Hoeber. Ordained as Deacon, by Bishop W. H. Van Vleck, Nov. 16. In 1853, called to Lebanon, Pa., where he served almost seven years. In 1858 the Church at Lebanon was burned, and a new one built the following year. In May, 1860, called to Nazareth, where he was the beloved pastor until his death. During his pastorate the new church was erected.

749. **Cecilia Henrietta Miksch,** m.n. Clewell. xviii, n. 11. May 22. Daughter of Joseph Clewell. Born Jan. 16, 1815. Married Richard Miksch, April 29, 1845. She had five children, three sons and two daughters, a son and a daughter preceding her into eternity.

750. **Caroline Sophia Kiefer,** m.n. Seyfried. xviii, n. 12. Aug. 15. Daughter of John Seyfried. Born Dec. 14, 1844. Married William Kiefer, Dec. 26, 1861. Had two children.

751. **Harrison Joseph Kiefer.** xviii, n. 12. Aug. 18. Infant son of William and Caroline Kiefer. Buried in the same grave with the mother.

752. **Albert Henry Miksch.** xxiv, s. 2. Sept. 24. Son of Richard and Cecilia (Clewell) Miksch. Aged 15 years.

753. **Christina Brunner.** xviii, n. 13. Oct. 1. Born Sept. 6, 1779, in Gnadenthal.

754. **Mary Barbara Henry,** m.n. Albright. xviii, n. 14. March 5, 1842. Daughter of Henry Albright and wife of William Henry, Sr. She had been buried in Scranton. Re-interred at Nazareth, Nov. 6, 1864.

755. **Alice Jane Kiefer.** xix, n. 6. Nov. 24. Daughter of William and Caroline (Seyfried) Kiefer.

756. **Levin Henry Wietsche.** xxv, s. 2. Dec. 17. Son of Carl and Catharine Wietsche. Aged 5 years. Diphtheria.

1865.

757. **Charles Herman Wietsche.** xxv, s. 3. Jan. 3. Son of Carl and Catharine Wietsche. Aged 7 years. Diphtheria. (The only children.)

758. **Catharine Elizabeth Kram.** xviii, n. 15. Feb. 17. Daughter of John Kram. Aged 28 years.

759. **James Benjamin Clewell.** xxiv, s. 3. Feb. 17. Son of Benjamin and Augusta Rondthaler Clewell. Aged 16 years.

760. **Anna Maria Fredericka Christ,** m.n. Danke. xviii, n. 16. March 16. Daughter of Franz Christian and Susannah (Ehrenhard) Danke. Born Feb. 20, 1822. Married Richard Christ. She had three sons, one of whom preceded her into eternity.

761. **Charles Frederick Vogler.** xxiv, s. 4. March 19. A pupil in Nazareth Hall, son of Brother Jesse Vogler, missionary among the Indians in Canada. He entered the Hall in 1863. Aged 12 years.

762. **John Lewis Miller.** xxiv, s. 5. April 1. Son of Lucinda Amelia Beck Born Jan. 6, 1842. Served in the army; was imprisoned at Libbey, Salisbury, etc. Returned home very ill.

763. **Henry Matthias Schultz.** xxiii, s. 14. April 30. Son of Samuel and Maria Christina (Peisert) Schultz. Born in Bethlehem, Oct. 15, 1828. Married June 25, 1851, Emma Angelina Clewell. Seven children survived.

764. **Cyrus L. Kram.** xxv, s. 4. June 6. Infant son of Catharine Kram.

765. **Augusta Octavia Mendenhall, m.n. Kern.** xviii, n. 17. June 30. Daughter of Andrew G. and Louisa (Levering) Kern. Born April 26, 1834. Married William P. Mendenhall, in Salem, N.C. March 15, 1860. Died in Dublin, Ind. Remains brought to Nazareth for interment.

766. **Beatus Haman.** xxv, s. 5. July 6. Infant son of Jacob J. Haman.

767. **Annie Elizabeth Beitel.** xix, n. 7. July 28. Infant daughter of Edward and Ebisene Beitel. Born Aug. 25, 1864.

768. **Frederick George Washington Meyers.** xxv, s. 6. Aug. 22. Infant son of Ferd. and Matilda (Flammer) Meyers.

769. **Harry Eugene Heinzelman.** xxv, s. 7. Aug. 26. Infant son of Jacob and Mary (Roesch) Heinzelman.

770. **Philip Walter, M.D.** xxiii, s. 15. Dec. 19. Born Sept. 10, 1799, in Upper Milford Township, Lehigh Co., Pa. Studied medicine with Dr. Green, in Quakertown. Physician in Lehigh County. In 1824 came to Nazareth, after having married Rachel B. Sellers in Whitemarsh. In 1826 united with the congregation, of which he was an exemplary member. Died very suddenly of heart disease.

771. **William F. Rauch.** xxiii, s. 16. Dec. 21. Born in Lititz, Oct. 24, 1822. Married Emma E. Peissert in Bethlehem. After having been in business for some time in Lebanon, Pa., moved to Nazareth in 1845. He was President of the Board of Trustees, and Postmaster. He had two sons, one of whom preceded the father into eternity.

1866.

772. **Eugene Benjamin Christ.** xxiv, s. 6. Jan. 9. Son of Richard and Fredericka (Danke) Christ. Born Nov. 13, 1846.

773. **Beatus Haas.** xxv, s. 8. Jan. 29. Son of Robert and Elizabeth Haas.

774. **John Samuel Haman.** xxiii, s. 17. Feb. 18. Born Jan. 30, 1788, on the Island of Barbadoes, W.I., where his parents were missionaries. In 1794 came, with his brother Adam, to Nazareth Hall. Later was in the Brethren's House, to learn a trade. In 1808 teacher in Nazareth Hall, remaining three years. Married Sarah Schmick, June 16, 1811, and took charge of the congregation Hotel, where he continued twenty-five years. Then carried on business of various kinds. He had five children, two of whom preceded him to eternity.

775. **Adelaide Maria Weber, m.n. Miksch.** xviii, n. 18. March 21. Daughter of Jacob and Catharine Miksch. Born Jan. 20, 1825. Married the widower, John August Weber, of Lebanon, Pa., March 24, 1863. Died in Lebanon. Remains brought to Nazareth for interment.

776. **John August Weber.** xxiii, s. 18. March 26. Born in Lauban, Prussia, May 19, 1809. When 18 years old went to Herrnhut to learn his trade. Later to Christiansfeld. Married Laura Christina Sophia Christoph, of

Christiansfeld, in Herrnhut, Feb. 25, 1834. In 1853 came to United States and lived in Lebanon. Here his wife and two children died. Married Adelaide Miksch in Nazareth. Died here, when about to bury his wife.

777. **Franz Joseph Nieth.** xxvi, s. 1. May 1. Born in Germany, March 19, 1785. Confirmed in the Catholic Church. Married Maria Anna Spraul, March 14, 1814. Their married life continued more than fifty-three years. In 1832 came to the United States, and lived near Nazareth. He had ten children, a son and a daughter preceding him to eternity.

778. **John Kram.** xxvi, s. 2. May 10. Born in Saucon Township, July 17, 1791. Confirmed in the Reformed Church. Married Rebecca Roth, Nov. 8, 1818. In 1841 moved to Old Nazareth, to one of the congregation farms, where he continued for eleven years. In 1856 united with the Church. Of his ten children four died before their father. During the last portion of his life, he was a great sufferer, being paralyzed. Aged 74 years.

779. **Ernestine Charlotte Lichtenthaeler,** m.n. Kitchelt. xxiii, n. 1. July 19. Born Aug. 31, 1807, in Emmaus, St. John, W.I., where her parents were missionaries. She came to Bethlehem when she was a small child. When 17 years old, entered Linden Hall Seminary as teacher; later in Bethlehem Seminary, and then in the family of Mr. William Henry. Married Christian Lichtenthaeler in Bethlehem, Aug. 1, 1837, and lived in Ephrata, Lancaster County, Pa., until they received a call as missionaries. Served in St. Kitts three years and in Antigua three years. Returned to the United States, and after some time spent in Nazareth and Bethlehem, served, with her husband, in Camden Valley, N.Y., and in Lebanon. Her husband then left the service of the Church and died in Chicago. His widow came to Nazareth, serving as teacher in the Parochial School six years. She had four children.

780. **Beatus Bardill.** xxv, s. 9. August 1. Son of Henry and Sophia Bardill.

781. **Margaret Schmidt.** xxiii, n. 2. Sept. 8. Born in Switzerland. She did not belong to the Church.

782. **Carrie Luanna Ettwein.** xix, n. 8. Oct. 15. Infant daughter of Jacob and Sophia (Miksch) Ettwein.

783. **Agnes Brigitta Brickenstein.** xxiv, n. 1. Oct. 26. Daughter of the Rev. J. C. and Sophia (Albright) Brickenstein. Born in Bethlehem, May 20, 1846. She served for some time as teacher in Bethlehem Seminary.

784. **Carl Heinrich Schneebeli.** xxv, s. 10. Nov. 22. Son of A. Schneebeli.

785. **Henry Emery Culp.** xxvi, s. 3. Nov. 22. Born in Philadelphia, June 20, 1831. Married Balvina Cuspo in 1853. His wife died in 1859. He had a daughter. In 1863 came to Nazareth, and Sept. 1, 1864, married Ellen Sellers. Baptized, as adult, Nov. 6, 1864. He had one daughter by this marriage. Died very suddenly in Easton.

786. **Constantia Florentine Culp.** xix, n. 9. Nov. 22. Daughter of Henry Culp. Born in Jacksonville, Florida, Oct. 5, 1854. Died on the same day as her father, and buried at the same time with him.

787. **Henrietta Stotz,** m.n. Ernst. xxiii, n. 3. Dec. 12. Born Jan 16, 1808, in Plainfield Township. Married Joseph Stotz, Dec. 26, 1826. She had six children, three of whom preceded her into eternity.

1867.

788. **Maria Elizabeth Miksch**, m.n. Rothrock. xxiii, n. 4. Jan. 2. Born in Springfield Township, Bucks Co., Pa., April 17, 1781. Served in Bethlehem; amongst the rest in the family of Brother Loskiel. Married Paul Miksch in Bethlehem. Lived in Christianspring. Her husband died in 1836. She had five children, three of whom died.

789. **Mary Francisca Grunewald.** xix, n. 10. Jan. 29. Daughter of Edward T. and Julia (Weber) Grunewald. Born March 27, 1863.

790. **Anna Maria Brunner.** xxiv, n. 2. Feb. 26. Born August 26, 1789. Spent nearly her entire life in the Sisters' House.

791. **Herman Otto Martin.** xxv, s. 11. April 13. Infant son of Herman and Caroline Martin.

792. **Florentine Clewell**, m.n. Leibert. xxiii, n. 5. May 28. Born near Emmaus, Feb. 24, 1816. Baptized at Emmaus by Brother Paul Weiss. After the death of her father, moved into the Sisters' House in Nazareth. Married Thomas Clewell, April 20, 1834. During the last fourteen years of her life, she was an invalid. She had eight children, one of whom preceded her into eternity.

793. **John Benjamin Soerensen.** xxiv, s. 7. June 25. Born in Ebersdorf, Oct. 18, 1805. Came to Nazareth thirty years ago. During the last twenty-seven years, he was employed in Nazareth Hall. A good, faithful man.

794. **Cecilia E. Clewell**, m.n. Haman. xxiii, n. 6. June 26. Daughter of John S. and Sarah (Schmick) Haman, and wife of Sidney A. Clewell. Born Dec. 20, 1814. Died in Philadelphia.

795. **Beatus Gerber.** xxv, s. 12. July 13. Son of John Gerber.

796. **Christian Henry Leibfried.** xxiv, s. 8. Aug. 21. Son of J. C. and Harriet Leibfried. Born Jan. 22, 1835. Served in the army from Sept., 1862, to July, 1863.

797. **Elizabeth Ricksecker**, m.n. King. xxiii, n. 7. Oct. 19. Born in Hope, N.J. June 14, 1786. Confirmed in Bethlehem. Married Jacob Ricksecker, Nov. 21, 1819, who died Aug. 1, 1844. Died at the home of her daughter, Mrs. Evans, at Hillmount.

798. **Emma Louisa Kram.** xxiv, n. 3. Dec. 16. Born April 20, 1846. Baptized by her uncle, the Rev. Dr. Hoffeditz.

1868.

799. **Beata Kern.** xix, n. 11. Jan. 7. Infant daughter of William and Marietta Kern.

800. **Carl Heinrich Leander Wietsche.** xxvi, s. 4. April 5. Born in Prussia, Feb. 9, 1815. Came to the United States in 1850. Married Catharine Hilberg, in 1855. He had two sons, both of whom died in their childhood.

801. **Elmer Frederick Fenner.** xxv, s. 13. May 5. Son of Wm. Fenner.

802. **George Schmidt.** xxvi, s. 5. May 6. Born in Forks Township, March 2, 1808. Confirmed in Nazareth, 1838. Married 1831.

803. **Rebecca Kingkinger**, m.n. Cassler. xxiii, n. 8. May 13. Born near Nazareth, Nov. 28, 1808. Confirmed in the Reformed Church at Dryland. Married Daniel Kingkinger in 1830. In 1840 united with the Schoeneck congregation. Her husband died June 7, 1859. She had eight children, three of whom preceded their mother into eternity.

804. **Annie Augusta Hartmann.** xix, n. 12. May 17. Daughter of C. Fredr. and Adelaide (Clewell) Hartmann.

805. **Catharine Elizabeth Bardill,** m.n. Schneider. xxiii, n. 9. May 24. Born March 16, 1790, in Old Nazareth. Her parents were Samuel and Catharine (Schmidt) Schneider. Married George Bardill, Nov. 9, 1813. She had four children, one of whom died. Husband died May 16, 1859.

806. **Edith Jane Rider.** xix, n. 13. June 7. Daughter of Alex. K. and Isabelle (Jones) Rider. Born in Poultney, Vermont.

807. **Maggie Ottilia Troeger.** xix, n. 14. July 21. Daughter of Henry Alex. and Ottilia Rosalia (Martin) Troeger. Born in Illinois, where the parents resided.

808. **Charles de Chamant.** xxvi, s. 6. July 25. Born in New Orleans. Son of Charles LeRoy de Chamant. Dead body found on the sidewalk of hotel, having probably fallen from the window during the night. Aged 33 years.

809. **John Andrew Haas.** xxv, s. 14. July 25. Infant son of Robert and Elizabeth (Lind) Haas.

810. **Henry Schneebeli.** xxv, s. 15. August 19. Infant son of Adolph and Louisa Fredericka Emilie Schneebeli.

811. **William Henry Werner.** xxvi, s. 7. Sept. 17. Son of Jonas and Sabina (Moersch) Werner. Born Jan. 24, 1836, in Bushkill Township. Married Marietta Heim Sept. 29, 1859. In 1860 united with Moravian Church. Served in the 153d Pa. Regiment in the army. An accident caused his death. Four children, one of whom died.

1869.

812. **Obadiah Ambrose Edelman.** xxv, s. 16. Jan. 3. Infant son of William and Amelia (Gruber) Edelman. Born Oct. 19, 1868.

813. **Clarissa Louisa Donachy,** m.n. Kichline. xxiii, n. 10. Jan. 22. Daughter of Conrad and Eloisa (Sachsen) Kichline. Born Oct. 4, 1836. Married Thomas Donachy, April 17, 1859. Five children, two of whom died.

814. **Ebisene Beitel.** xxiii, n. 11. March 1. Daughter of Aaron and Mary (Schweitzer) Babp. Born April 27, 1834, in Forks Township. Her father died when she was in her eleventh year. Married Edward Beitel, Dec. 24, 1857. She had five children, two of whom preceded her into eternity.

815. **Sallie Zimmerman Walter.** xxiv, n. 4. March 2. Daughter of Dr. Philip and Emma (Link) Walter. Born March 15 1857.

816. **John Schmidt.** xxvi, s. 8. April 15. Son of Franz and Elizabeth Schmidt. Born July 9, 1795. Married Catharine Sybilla Whitesell in 1818. He had four children, one son, Henry, surviving. Married Sophia Louisa Beck, Sept. 17, 1826. He had six children.

817. **William Alexander Schaefer.** xxiv, s. 9. May 31. Son of Solomon and Wilhelmina Adelaide (Giersch) Schaefer. Born Aug. 2, 1835.

818. **William Beitel.** xxvi, s. 9. Aug. 26. Son of John and Magdalene (Romig) Beitel. Born Oct. 19, 1814. Married Eliza Ann Ruch, Nov. 26, 1837. Merchant and prominent citizen and officer of the Church, highly respected. He had four children; three sons and a daughter, one son surviving.

819. **Maria Ettwein,** m.n. McRady. xxiii, n. 12. Sept. 11. Born in Bethlehem Township, Aug. 20, 1790; a member of the Lutheran Church. Married

John Ettwein, grandson of Bishop Ettwein, June 24, 1810. She had four sons and three daughters. Husband died May 20, 1848.

820. **Jacob Bolliger.** xxvi, s. 10. Nov. 4. Born in Switzerland, Jan. 27, 1813. His parents were members of the Diaspora congregation. He united with the congregation in Königsfeld in 1848. He also lived in Gnadau and Kleinwelka. In 1852 came to United States, living in Nazareth. Married Caroline Baehrens, Nov. 26, 1854. He was a very pious man.

821. **Beata Schneebeli.** xix, n. 15. Nov. 18. Infant daughter of A. Schneebeli.

822. **Eugene Francis Miksch.** xxv, s. 17. Nov. 26. Infant son of Charles and Maria (Kiefer) Miksch.

823. **Mary Bute,** m.n. Bardill. xxiii, n. 13. Dec. 11. Daughter of John and Anna Barbara Bardill. Born in Bethlehem Nov. 14, 1799. Married George H. Bute, April 7, 1825. Nov. 23, 1828, they were called as missionaries to Paramaribo, S. A. In 1831 returned, on account of impaired health. 1832 lived in Philadelphia. In 1838 moved to Nazareth. She had four children, one of whom survived.

1870.

824. **Jacob Gallmeyer.** xxvi, s. 11. March 24. Born June 15, 1802, in Ebersheim, Rhine Baiern. His second wife was Anna Becker. Had nine children, of whom three survived. Wife died in 1848.

825. **Lillie May Kiefer.** xix, n. 16. March 29. Twin daughter of William R. and Maria Kiefer.

826. **Emma Louisa Seyfried.** xix, n. 17. May 31. Daughter of Levin S. and Sarah Ann (Levers) Seyfried. Born Dec. 21, 1868.

827. **Edmund Jacob Lehr.** xxvi, s. 12. July 18. Son of Edmund Jacob and Angelina (Lucas) Lehr. Born in Saucon Township, Oct. 30, 1846. Died in Nazareth Hall, where his mother was sick-nurse.

828. **John Beitel.** xxvi, s. 13. Aug. 1. Born July 18, 1782, in Nazareth, and baptized the following day by Brother Lembke. His parents were John and Julianna (Schmidt) Beitel. Married Anna Magdalene Romig, of Emmaus, April 23, 1810. She died Aug. 9, 1849, and had six children. Married Lydia Hasselberger, m.n. Bauer, Oct. 11, 1850. He was postmaster twenty-eight years. He did much to beautify and improve the graveyard.

829. **Bernard Francis Schaefer.** xxiv, s. 10. Sept. 20. Son of Solomon and Anna (Luckenbach) Schaefer. Born Jan. 31, 1853.

830. **Beatus Baker.** xxv, s. 18. Oct. 20.

831. **Anna Rebecca Stout,** m.n. Miksch. xxiii, n. 14. Nov. 10. Daughter of Nathaniel and Anna Maria (Fritsch) Miksch. Born Aug. 11, 1788. Married Peter Stout, Sept. 23, 1810. Husband died Oct. 7, 1845. She had two sons and five daughters, all surviving their mother. During the last fifteen years she lived in the Sisters' House, with her daughter Sophia. Died suddenly during the night.

832. **Beatus Beitel.** xxvii, s. 1. Dec. 14. Son of John F. and Ida (Miksch) Beitel.

1871.

833. **William Joseph Martin.** xxvii, s. 2. Jan. 5. Infant son of Otto Martin.

834. **Ellen Sophia Abel.** xix, n. 18. Jan. 13. Daughter of Lewis and Elmira (Clewell) Abel. Born May 3, 1864.

835. **Jacob Clewell.** xxvi, s. 14. Jan. 30. Son of John and Anna Johanna (Klein) Clewell; born Oct. 11, 1799. Married Anna Rebecca Seyfried, who had eight children, of whom two sons and two daughters survived. His wife died June 15, 1859. In 1864 he married Emilie Eliza Grunewald, m.n. Bardill. For forty-eight years he was a member of the trombone choir.

836. **Henry Cuthbert Gaw.** xxiv, s. 11. March 2. Pupil in Nazareth Hall. Born in Philadelphia, March 27, 1857. Entered the Hall, Sept., 1870.

837. **Christian David Busse.** xxvi, s. 15. April 2. Son of Andrew and Anna Christina (Busch) Busse. Born Nov. 13, 1789, in Gnadenthal, where his father was minister and pastor in Nazareth and member of the Provincial Board. He was educated in Nazareth Hall. After learning a trade, lived in York. Returning to Nazareth, he married Marie Theresa Reinke, daughter of the pastor at Nazareth, April 24, 1814. He had four children, of whom one daughter preceded him into eternity. Married Mary Christina Rauch in Bethlehem, Feb. 8, 1824. He had three children, of whom a daughter died. He was an officer of the Church, delegate to Synods, and Justice of the Peace forty-three years.

838. **Thomas Clewell.** xxvi, s. 16. April 13. Son of John and Anna Johanna (Klein) Clewell. Born Nov. 3, 1802. Married Florentine Leibert, April 20, 1834. He had four sons and four daughters; one son preceded him into eternity.

839. **Beatus Seyfried.** xxvii, s. 3. June 16. Infant son of Levin and Sarah (Levers) Seyfried.

840. **Emma Amelia Rauch.** xxiii, n. 15. Aug. 19. Daughter of Christian and Sarah Peissert. Born near Schoeneck, Sept. 22, 1823. Married William F. Rauch, who died Dec. 21, 1865. She had two sons, one of whom died before the mother.

841. **Lisetta Amelia Luckenbach.** xxiv, n. 5. Sept 2. Born near Bethlehem, Oct. 12, 1801. Educated at Lititz. In 1816 moved to Nazareth and in 1825 into the Sisters' House, where she was sick-nurse from 1830 to 1844.

842. **Robert Samuel Peters.** xxvii, s. 4. Dec. 9. Son of Joseph and Mary Ellen Peters, m.n. Lynn. Born in Plainfield Township, Nov. 29, 1871.

843. **William Julius Nitzsche.** xxvii, s. 5. Dec. 22. Son of August and Ellen (Venter) Nitzsche.

1872.

844. **Anna Joanna Eckensberger.** xxiii, n. 16. Jan. 25. Daughter of John and Anna Joanna (Klein) Clewell; born May 12, 1786. Married widower John Jacob Eckensberger, April 7, 1817, with whom she lived forty-two years. Husband died May 13, 1859.

845. **Daniel Riegel.** xxvi, s. 17. Feb. 24. Born in Lower Saucon Township, March 15, 1804. Married Hannah Weaver, who died Feb. 23, 1855. He was landlord of the Hotel for many years. Survived by eight children.

846. **Ellen Jane George.** xxiv, n. 6. March 6. Daughter of Reuben and Mary Elizabeth (Knauss) George. Born in Georgetown, Aug. 30, 1859.

847. **Louisa Caroline Venter.** xxi, n. 1. April 4. Daughter of Emanuel and Cornelia (Cope) Venter. Born March 25, 1872.

848. **Magdalena Schmidt,** m.n. Ziegenthaler. xxiii, n. 17. April 23. Born in Berne, Switzerland, Feb., 1780. In 1825 came with her husband to this country.

849. **Francis William Knauss.** xxvi, s. 18. July 15. (Minister.) Son of Saml. Lewis and Jane Knauss. Born in Bethlehem, Dec. 9, 1840. Entered Theological Seminary in 1862. Teacher in Nazareth Hall 1864. A year later went to Hope, Ind., where he assisted Brother Edwin T. Senseman, the pastor. Having been called as pastor to Moravia, Iowa, he was ordained by Bishop David Bigler, in Lancaster. He married Caroline Dizinger, of Philadelphia, May 15, 1866. He remained at Moravia five years. He was ordained as Presbyter, by Bishop H. A. Shultz, Nov. 25, 1868. He was obliged by failing health to retire from service in July, 1871.

850. **Augusta Fredericka H. Warman,** m.n. Bird. xxv, n. 1. August 13. Born in Gracefield, Ireland, where her father, Thomas Bird, was pastor of the Moravian Church, Oct. 23, 1817. He died at Malmsbury, England. She then went to Fulneck to school. She was teacher in Duckenfield, near Manchester; later in Ireland was governess in the family of the Rev. Samuel O'Sullivan. Married John F. Warman, Feb., 1842. In May, 1849, came to the United States, and lived fifteen years in New York. Then she served on the Indian Mission in Canada, where her husband was missionary; then at Olney, Ill., and finally at Nazareth. She had four children, of whom two survived.

851. **Rebecca Hoeber,** m.n. Clewell. xxv, n. 2. Oct. 20. Born in Schoeneck, April 28, 1801. Her parents died during the same week, when she was in her fifteenth year. She then moved into the Nazareth Sisters' House. Married Christian Renatus Hoeber, Aug. 29, 1823. She had two sons and four daughters; a son and a daughter preceded her into eternity.

852. **Johanna Louisa Miksch.** xxiv, n. 7. Nov. 27. Daughter of Paul and Maria Elizabeth Miksch. Unmarried. Born June 24, 1813.

853. **Lucia Ottilia Martin,** m.n. Kuehle. xxv, n. 3. Dec. 24. Born in Vienna, Austria, Nov. 7, 1804. Married Christian Frederick Martin, April, 1825, and moved to Neukirchen, in Vogtland. In 1833 came to the United States, and after living five years in New York, moved to Cherry Hill and later to Nazareth. She was a good musician, harpist and singer. She had seven children. Three daughters preceded her into eternity.

854. **Sophia Henrietta Senseman,** m.n. Reichel. xxv, n. 4. Dec. 28. Daughter of the Rev. G. B. Reichel. Born in Salem, N. C., March 5, 1822. Her mother died when she was only seven years old, and about five years later, her father died. In 1834 her stepmother moved to Bethlehem, with seven children, and soon after Mrs. Senseman was adopted into the family of her uncle, Bro. C. F. Seidel. She was educated in the Young Ladies' Seminary at Bethlehem, where she later served as teacher. Married Comenius Senseman, of Nazareth, in May, 1847. She had two children; a son died some years previous to his mother's death.

1873.

855. **William Edward Beitel.** xxvii, s. 6. Feb. 12. Son of Edward and Ebisene (Babp) Beitel. Born Aug. 8, 1867.

856. **Christian Frederick Martin.** xxviii, s. 1. Feb. 16. Born in Neukirchen, Saxony, Jan. 31, 1796. Married Lucia Ottilia Kuehle, April, 1825. In Sept., 1833, came to New York, carrying on his business as guitar-maker.

6

Then moved to Cherry Hill, and twenty-three years later moved to Nazareth. He was the most celebrated and best guitar-maker in the United States, and carried on the business quite extensively. He was a pious and very benevolent man, greatly respected and beloved. His wife died Dec. 24, 1872.

857. **Delilah Neumeyer,** m.n. Engler. xxv, n. 5. June 9. Born in Lower Nazareth Township, Sept. 14, 1846. Married Henry Neumeyer Feb. 17, 1867. One son survived.

858. **Beata Beitel.** xxi, n. 2. April 9. Infant daughter of Edward and Angelica (Kern) Beitel.

859. **Beatus Henry.** xxvii, s. 7.

860. **Lilah Catharine Messinger.** xxi, n. 3. June 20. Infant daughter of Aaron and Louisa (Wenhold) Messinger. Born Sept. 11, 1872.

861. **Anna Sophia Brickenstein,** m.n. Albright. xxv, n. 6. Sept. 2. Daughter of Henry and Anna Barbara (Hubley) Albright. Born in Lititz, June 25, 1810. Married the Rev. John C. Brickenstein, in 1830, who was called as pastor to Emmaus, Pa. Later Warden in Bethlehem. Then moved to Middlesex County, Virginia. Returned to Nazareth, and, during several years, boarded the Theological students at Ephrata, Brother Brickenstein being assistant professor. She had eight children, five of whom survived their mother.

862. **Reuben George.** xxviii, s. 2. Sept. 9. Son of Daniel and Catharine George. Born Nov. 28, 1826. Married Mary Elizabeth Knauss, Jan. 8, 1855. Received into the Church at Nazareth in 1871. He had nine children, eight of whom survived.

863. **Robert Constantine Haas.** xxvii, s. 8. Nov. 4. Son of Robert and Elizabeth (Lind) Haas. Born April 23, 1865.

864. **Lewis Edward Abel.** xxvii, s. 9. Nov. 29. Son of Lewis and Elmira (Clewell) Abel. Born June 7, 1871.

1874.

865. **Henrietta Theresa Venter,** m.n. Roeder. xxv, n. 7. Jan. 10. Born in Lobenstein, Germany, Oct. 10, 1800. Married John Henry Venter in 1821, with whom she lived 52 years. In 1834 came to the United States, living in Nazareth, Philadelphia and Nazareth, in the latter place forty years. She had twelve children, five of whom died in Germany. Two sons and four daughters survived.

866. **Charles Frederick Reichel.** xxiv, s. 12. April 10. Son of the Rev. Edward H. and Charlotte E. (Meas) Reichel. Born in Nazareth, June 26, 1855.

867. **John Seyfried.** xxviii, s. 3. May 6. Son of Nicholas and Susanna (Ehrenhard) Seyfried. Born in Plainfield Township, June 22, 1792. Married Anna Maria Eyerly, March 29, 1813. He had six sons and three daughters. His wife died July 27, 1838. Married Rebecca Kind, March 3, 1844. He had one daughter by this marriage. Of his ten children, five preceded him into eternity.

868. **Sophia Louisa Schmidt,** m.n. Beck. xxv, n. 8. May 14. Daughter of Christian Henry and Anna Christina (Eyerly) Beck. Born in Nazareth, June 22, 1800. Married the widower, John Schmidt, Sept. 17, 1826. Her husband died, April 16, 1869. She had two sons and four daughters.

869 **Beatus Messinger.** xxvii, s. 10. May 15.

870. **Ernst Leonard Bachschmidt.** xxiv, s. 13. Aug. 19. Son of Paul and Ida Bachschmidt. Born in Nazareth, July 17, 1855. He was drowned in the Bushkill, while here on a visit from New York, where he was studying as architect.

871. **Charles Christian Brown.** xxiv, s. 14. Nov. 1. Son of Daniel and Lucinda (Ebbeke) Brown. Born Nov. 17, 1854.

872. **Andrew Gottfried Kern.** xxviii, s. 4. Dec. 25. Son of John Michael and Anna Maria (Stott) Kern. Born in Nazareth, Sept. 7, 1793. Married Catharine Louisa Levering, Feb. 21, 1819, with whom he had eight children. His wife died Jan. 13, 1837. In Oct., 1837, married Sarah Lichtenthaeler, with whom he had four children. He was a highly respected member of the Church, in which he held important offices for many years. During the latter part of his life, he was deeply interested in the history of the Church, and made many researches of importance. He was one of the first members of the Moravian Historical Society.

1875.

873. **John Stotz.** xxiv, s. 15. Jan. 20. Son of Joseph and Anna Julianna (Eigenbrod) Stotz. Born Aug. 16, 1812.

874. **Matilda Elizabeth Kern.** xxi, n. 5. Feb. 16. Infant daughter of Julius Alexander and Catharine (Oplinger) Kern.

875. **Elizabeth Bauer.** xxiv, n. 8. March 16. A member of the Lutheran Church.

876. **Caroline Maria Schultz,** m.n. Warg. xxv, n. 9. April 25. Born in Bethlehem Township, Jan. 30, 1825. Married Levi Jacob Schultz, March 30, 1851. She had five children, of whom two died.

877. **Joseph Straub.** xxviii, s. 5. May 4. Born in Kappel, Würtemberg, Feb. 2, 1815. Came to the United States in 1854, and to Nazareth in 1860. He had two sons and a daughter.

878. **Julia Grunewald,** m.n. Weaver. xxv, n. 10. July 25. Daughter of Jacob and Margaret (Reimer) Weaver, born in Easton, Oct. 6, 1840. Confirmed in the Moravian Church. Married Edward T. Grunewald, Sept. 29, 1859. She had a daughter, who died.

879. **Amanda Clara Catharine Kern.** xxiv, n. 9. Aug. 1. Daughter of Peter and Matilda Louisa Kern. Born July 16, 1851.

880. **Joseph Giersch.** xxviii, s. 6. Aug. 19. Son of Christian and Elizabeth Giersch. Born in Nazareth, April 19, 1785. In 1809 married Judith Meinung, of Salem, N. C., and moved to Filetown. In 1824 to Philadelphia. His wife died in 1844. After residing in Philadelphia forty-seven years, moved to Nazareth in Sept., 1871. He had nine children, of whom five preceded him into eternity.

881. **John Henry Venter.** xxviii, s. 7. Sept. 10. Son of John Andrew and Eleanora (Trautwein) Venter. Born in Mühlhausen, Germany, Jan. 2, 1795. In 1821 married Henrietta Theresa Roeder. In 1834 arrived in the United States. He lived in Nazareth, Philadelphia and Nazareth. He had twelve children, of whom five died in Germany.

882. **Richard Francis Miksch.** xxviii, s. 8. Oct. 14. Son of Nathaniel and Julianna Miksch. Born March 8, 1816. Married Cecilia Henrietta Clewell,

April 29, 1845, who died May 22, 1864. He had five children, three sons and two daughters. A son and a daughter preceded him into eternity. Married Caroline L. Kreider, of Lititz, April 29, 1869.

883. **Beatus Kern.** xxvii, s. 11. Dec. 14. Infant son of Edward and Maria Kern.

884. **Christina Augusta Clewell,** m.n. Rondthaler. xxv, n. 11. Dec. 25. Daughter of Emanuel and Maria Christina Rondthaler. Born in York, Pa., where her father was pastor, Feb. 24, 1810. Married Benjamin Clewell, Sept. 16, 1830. She had six children, three of whom preceded her into eternity.

1876.

885. **George Henry Bute, M.D.** xxviii, s. 9. Feb. 13. Born at Brommershob, Germany, May 20, 1792. In order to avoid enlistment in the French army, he left and went to sea for several years on Dutch vessels. Being left at Genoa, he traveled on foot to Germany and set sail for America. He landed in Philadelphia in Aug., 1819. He was a teacher in Nazareth Hall from 1822 to 1823. In April, 1825, married Mary Bardill and moved to Philadelphia. In 1828 called as missionary to Surinam, S.A. On account of impaired health, he returned to this country. He became a Homeopathic physician, and was very successful, particularly during the prevalence of Asiatic cholera in Philadelphia. He moved to Nazareth. Two of his daughters died in 1851. His wife died in December, 1869.

886. **Beata Koken.** xxi, n. 6. March 26.

887. **Caroline Leibert.** xxiv, n. 10. Sept. 3. Daughter of the Rev. Eugene and Sarah (Zorn) Leibert, principal of Nazareth Hall. Born in Sharon, Ohio, April 9, 1860.

888. **Cornelia Louisa Messinger.** xxi, n. 7. Dec. 11. Infant daughter of Aaron and Louisa (Wenhold) Messinger.

1877.

889. **Alfred Eugene Sondermann.** xxvii, s. 12. Jan. 7. Infant son of the Rev. Theodore Sondermann, pastor of the German Church in New York.

890. **Julianne Emilie Kern,** m.n. Danke. xxv, n. 12. Feb. 9. Born March 16, 1816. In 1841 she married Edwin F. Clewell, in Schoeneck. She had a child, which died in its infancy. Her husband died in 1845. Married Gustav A. Kern thirteen years later.

891. **Beata Rice.** xxi, n. 8. March 14. Daughter of the Rev. W. Henry and Mary E. (Holland) Rice.

892. **Maurice Christian Kern.** xxiv, s. 16. March 21. Eldest son of William H. and Lucinda (Ebbeke) Kern. Born Sept. 8, 1852.

893. **Emma Gertrude Werner.** xxi, n. 9. April 10. Daughter of William H. and Lucetta E. Werner. Born June 22, 1871.

894. **Mary Elizabeth Beck.** xxiv, n. 11. May 11. Daughter of Jacob and Lydia (Nolf) Beck. Born Dec. 16, 1855. She was a teacher in the Public School and in the Sunday-school.

895. **William Franklin Schultz.** xxviii, s. 10. August 6. Son of Levi J. and Caroline (Warg) Schultz. Born May 24, 1853. He was married Christmas Day, 1875, to Mary Ellen Woodring.

896. **Clara Angelica Eichman**, m.n. Schmidt. xxv, n. 13. Aug. 28. Wife of Emanuel Eichman. Born Sept. 17, 1841. Married Dec. 2, 1866.

897. **Edward Henry Reichel.** xxviii, s. 11. Sept. 7. Son of Gotthold Benjamin and Henrietta Fredericka (Vierling) Reichel. (His father died Dec. 20, 1834.) Born in Salem, N.C., Aug. 11, 1820. Educated at Nazareth Hall and the Theological Seminary. In 1849 married Charlotte Elizabeth Meas. Occupied the position of pastor in New York, during the absence of Brother David Bigler at the General Synod of 1848 ; and later, for a brief time, served as assistant to Brother Emanuel Rondthaler, in Philadelphia. Called as pastor to Camden Valley, N.Y. Principal of Nazareth Hall, from 1854 to 1866, when he retired on account of impaired health. Died very suddenly of heart disease. He had three children, a son having preceded him into eternity.

898. **Beatus Beil.** xxvii, s. 13. Nov. 22. Infant son of M. and Mary J. (Gruber) Beil.

1878.

899. **Clara L. Shive.** xxi, n. 10. Jan. 27. Daughter of William H. and Emma (Gramlich) Shive.

900. **Mary A. Heller**, m.n. Seyfried. xxv, n. 14. April 8. Daughter of Philip and Anna (Gambold) Seyfried. Born Nov. 16, 1818. Married John Heller in 1837. She had six children, two sons dying before their mother.

901. **Mary Elizabeth Bates.** xxiv, n. 12. May 3. Daughter of Harvey and Harriet (Danke) Bates. Born in Monroe County, April 2, 1856. When only four years old, became a member of the family of Gustav A. and Emilie Kern, the latter being her aunt. She was a teacher in the Sunday-school.

902. **Maria Anna Nieth**, m.n. Spraul. xxv, n. 15. July 10. Born in Baden, Oct. 24, 1791. Married Franz Joseph Nieth, March 24, 1814. Came to the United States in 1832. Husband died May 1, 1866. She had ten children, of whom two preceded her into eternity. Aged 86 years.

903. **Jacob Miksch.** xxviii, s. 12. Oct. 24. Son of John Christian and Anna Philippina (Loesch) Miksch. Born in Christianspring, Aug. 24, 1787. Married Catharine Weinland, Feb. 5, 1812. On Feb. 5, 1862, they celebrated their golden wedding festival. His wife died Sept. 8, 1862. They had eight children, of whom two sons and a daughter preceded their parents into eternity. Father Miksch was the oldest member of the congregation.

904. **Rebecca Kram**, m.n. Roth. xxv, n. 16. Oct. 25. Born April 25, 1802. Married to John Kram, Nov. 8, 1818. In 1856 united with the Moravian Church. She had ten children, four of whom preceded their parents into eternity. Her husband died May 10, 1866.

1879.

905. **William Theodore Kern.** xxviii, s. 13. March 1. Son of Andrew G. and Catharine Louisa (Levering) Kern. Born June 26, 1824. Married Marietta Rilbert. During the latter part of his life he was a member of the Evangelical Church, having severed his connection with the Moravian Church.

906. **Caroline Elizabeth Morrish**, m.n. Lichtenthaeler. xxv, n. 17. March 31. Daughter of Brother Abraham and Charlotte (Kreiter) Lichtenthaeler, and

wife of Brother Alexander C. Morrish, missionary in the West Indies. Being in feeble health, she came to this country in the hope of recovering. Died here aged 35 years.

907. **Maria Louisa Hark,** m.n. Bute. xxvi, n. 1. March 31. Daughter of Dr. George H. and Mary (Bardill) Bute. Married Dr. Joseph Hark. She had five children, four sons and a daughter, the latter dying in infancy.

908. **Ellen Heller,** m.n. Santee. xxvi, n. 2. April 24. Wife of J. Monroe Heller. Born March 7, 1855. Married Nov. 10, 1877. She had one child.

909. **Robert Oliver Clewell.** xxiv, s. 17. April 30. Son of Henry and Eliza (Peissert) Clewell. Aged 16 years.

910. **Marietta Werner,** m.n. Heim. xxvi, n. 3. May 17. Married William H. Werner, Sept. 29, 1859. She had four children, one of whom died in infancy. Husband died Sept. 17, 1868. Aged 40 years.

911. **Catharine F. Beitel,** m.n. Tindall. xxvi, n. 8. June 5. Wife of Charles H. Beitel. Born in Brooklyn, Jan. 7, 1838. Died in Catasauqua. Re-interred here.

912. **J. Monroe Heller.** xxviii, s. 14. Sept. 22. Son of John and Maria (Seyfried) Heller. Born May 20, 1853. Married Ellen Santee, Nov. 10, 1877, who died April 24, 1879.

913. **Sarah Clewell.** xxiv, n. 13. Nov. 3. Daughter of John and Anna Johanna (Klein) Clewell. Born in Nazareth. The last survivor of a family of four sons and five daughters. Lived in the Sisters' House many years.

914. **William David Stout.** xxiv, s. 18. Nov. 12. Son of Peter and Anna Rebecca (Miksch) Stout. Born in Nazareth, Nov. 3, 1828. Served in the army.

915. **Benjamin Clewell.** xxviii, s. 15. Dec. 31. Son of Christian Frederick and Maria R. (Kreiter) Clewell. Born Nov. 10, 1804, in Niesky. Married Christina Augusta Rondthaler, Sept. 10, 1830. He had six children, three of whom preceded him into eternity. His wife died Dec. 25, 1875. He was an excellent musician, and was organist at Nazareth thirty-five years.

1880.

916. **Edward T. Beitel.** xxvii, s. 14. Jan. 8. Son of Charles H. and the late Catharine (Tindall) Beitel. Born at Cornwall on the Hudson, March 8, 1876. Died in Catasauqua.

917. **Amelia Sophia Whitesell,** m.n. Kichline. xxvi, n. 4. Jan. 6. Daughter of Conrad and Eloisa Kichline. Born March 22, 1838. Married Theodore Whitesell, April 4, 1861.

918. **Sarah Musselman,** m.n. Zimmerman. xxvi, n. 5. Jan. 15. Daughter of Adam and Sarah Zimmerman. Born in Philadelphia, May 15, 1807. Married Christian Musselman in Philadelphia, April 24, 1839. She had four children, all of whom died.

919. **John Christian Leibfried.** xxviii, s. 16. Jan. 31. Born in Würtemberg, Sept. 24, 1809. When six years old, came to this country with his parents. In 1830 he moved from Bethlehem to Nazareth. Married Harriet Beitel, daughter of Henry and Rosina Beitel. He had five children, two of whom preceded him to eternity.

920. **Charles Frederick Kluge.** xxviii, s. 17. March 26. Born July 21, 1801, at the Indian Mission Station on the White River, now Indiana, where his

parents were engaged as missionaries. His parents, with their little children, were obliged to flee from the station, enduring great hardships. Entered Nazareth Hall when in his seventh year, continuing there until 1817. Then he went to Salem, N.C., in order to complete the theological course of study under Brother Herman, there being no Theological Seminary at that time. Later he was teacher in the Parochial School at Salem for several years, and then teacher in Nazareth Hall from 1821 to 1828. Then called to conduct the Parochial School in Lancaster, Pa. Married Agnes M. von Pannach, in Bethlehem, Sept. 9, 1828. He was ordained as Deacon Nov. 14, 1830. Principal of Linden Hall Seminary, and pastor pro tem. at Lititz. 1836 pastor in New York. In 1839 Warden at Nazareth, temporarily. Principal of Nazareth Hall till 1844. Then Administrator at Salem. In 1848 delegate to General Synod, during which he was ordained Presbyter by Bishop Nitschmann. 1853 elected to the Unity's Elders' Conference. In 1857, declining a re-election, came to this country, living at Bethlehem and then at Nazareth. In 1878 celebrated golden wedding. Five children, all of whom survived him.

921. **Jeannette Ziegler**, m.n. Kahn. xxvi, n. 6. July 5. Born in 1817, in Obermosel, Rheinbaiern. Married George Ziegler, April 16, 1851, and came to this country. She had six children, four of whom survived her.

922. **Emily Beitel.** xxi, n. 11. Aug. 8. Daughter of Lewis and Mary E. (Arnold) Beitel. Born in Easton, Feb. 23, 1880.

923. **Emma Helena Beitel**, m.n. Boyer. xxvi, n. 7. Nov. 22. Daughter of John and Eliza Boyer. Born in Bath, Jan. 4, 1847. Married Richard O. Beitel, Feb. 27, 1873. United with Moravian Church, 1874.

1881.

924. **Christian Renatus Hoeber.** xxviii, s. 18. Jan. 19. Son of the Rev. Nicholas and Joanna Hoeber. Born July 17, 1802, in Bethel, Lebanon Co., Pa. In 1808, his father having been appointed warden at Nazareth, came here. Married Rebecca Clewell, Aug. 28, 1823. He was postmaster twelve years. In the Church he held the offices of "sacristan," or *diener*, trustee and elder. His wife died Oct. 20, 1872. He had six children, two of whom died in their infancy.

925. **William Albert Koken.** xxvii, s. 15. Jan. 31. Son of Jacob and Mary (Schultz) Koken. Born March 10, 1879.

926. **Solomon Schaefer.** xxix, s. 1. Mar. 28. Son of Daniel and Maria (Kratzer) Schaefer. Born in Lehigh Township, Sept. 3, 1812. In his nineteenth year, he moved to Nazareth, learning the saddler's trade with Christian Busse. He was a sacristan and trustee. Married Wilhelmina Adelaide Giersch, May 19, 1833, who died Feb. 19, 1842. There were four children by this marriage, two of whom died in childhood. Married Anna Luckenbach, at Bethlehem, Sept. 7, 1843. Five children, of whom only one son survived.

927. **Esther Nietzsche.** xxi, n. 12. Infant daughter of August Nietzsche.

928. **Mary Caroline Lennert.** xxiv, n. 14. July 18. Daughter of the Rev. William L. and Suzette (Fetter) Lennert. Born in Lebanon, Aug. 26, 1860. Died in Norristown Asylum.

929. **Agnes Florence Odenwelder.** xxi, n. 13. July 22. Infant daughter of Edwin and Jane Odenwelder. Born Jan. 3, 1881.

930. **David Warner.** xxix, s. 2. Aug. 27. Son of Massa and Dorothea (Miksch) Warner. Born in Bethlehem, Aug. 17, 1791. Married Esther Miller, April 5, 1818, with whom he lived sixty-three years. In 1832 moved to Nazareth, where they lived forty-eight years. They had three children, all of whom died in childhood.

931. **Daniel Ziegler.** xxix, s. 3. Sept. 12. Son of Daniel and Maria Ziegler. Born April 20, 1808. Married Anna Sponheimer in Jan., 1834. United with the Church in 1862.

932. **Franklin Thomas Kern.** xxvii, s. 16. Nov. 16. Son of Julius and Catharine Kern.

933. **Levi Jacob Schultz.** xxix, s. 4. Dec. 29. Son of Samuel and Christina Schultz. Born in Bethlehem, March 11, 1827. Married Caroline M. Warg, March 30, 1851. Two years later moved to Nazareth. In 1870 to a farm in the neighborhood. Wife died April 25, 1875. Five children, of whom three died. Married Mary C. Reese, Feb. 16, 1878. One child.

1882.

934. **Esther Warner,** m.n. Miller. xxvi, n. 9. Jan. 8. Daughter of G. and Salome Miller. The widow of David Warner, who died Aug. 27, 1881.

935. **Sophia Wilhelmina Stout.** xxiv, n. 15. Feb. 16. Daughter of Peter and Anna Rebecca (Miksch) Stout. Born May 12, 1816.

936. **Walter Lichtenthaeler Kern.** xxvii, s. 17. Feb. 22. Infant son of Edward and Maria (Clewell) Kern. Born Oct. 26, 1881.

937. **Caroline Lisetta Miksch,** m.n. Kreider. xxvi, n. 10 March 20. Daughter of Daniel and Mary (Lennert) Kreider. Born in Lititz, June 26, 1823. During nine years she was a teacher in Linden Hall Seminary. Married Richard Miksch, April 29, 1869. Her husband died Oct. 14, 1875.

938. **Francis Xavier Etschman.** xxix, s. 5. May 24. Son of Joseph and Francisca (Werber) Etschman. Born Feb. 23, 1823, in Etterheim, Baden. Came to the United States when young. Married Fredericka Augusta Venter, in Philadelphia, March 8, 1849, and soon after united with the Moravian Church. Moved to Bushkill Township, and then to Nazareth. Served in the army and was a prisoner at Libbey. In 1880 moved to Philadelphia. He had seven children, two of whom died before their father.

939. **Anna Ziegler,** m.n. Sponheimer. xxvi, n. 11. Sept. 27. Daughter of Lewis Sponheimer. Born in Plainfield Township, July 29, 1813. Married Daniel Ziegler, Jan., 1834, who died Sept. 12, 1881.

940. **Mary Christina Busse,** m.n. Rauch. xxvi, n. 12. Dec. 22. Born in Lititz, Nov. 23, 1793. Married the widower, Christian David Busse, Feb. 8, 1824, who died April 2, 1871. She had three children, one daughter preceded her into eternity.

1883.

941. **Rebecca Seyfried,** m.n. Kind. xxvi, n. 13. May 13. Born Sept. 3, 1812. Married John Seyfried, March 3, 1844, who died March 6, 1874. She had a daughter, who preceded her into eternity.

942. **Caroline Emma Shive.** xxi, n. 14. July 19. Daughter of William and Emma (Gramlich) Shive. Born in New York, March 19, 1882. Died in New York.

943. **Charles Sellers, M.D.** xxix, s. 6. Sept. 13. Son of Philip and Hannah Sellers. Born in Whitemarsh, Sept. 14, 1816. In his fourteenth year came to Nazareth, attending school in the Hall, and living with his sister, Mrs. Dr. P. Walter. Later he was engaged in business in Philadelphia. Illness obliged him to return to Nazareth, and he then studied medicine with Dr. Walter. Graduated at Jefferson College. Married Caroline Bardill, May 21, 1840. He was a skillful and esteemed physician for many years. During the last eight years he was paralytic. He, together with several others, successfully improved the graveyard, planting trees and shrubbery. He had two daughters.

1884.

944. **Aaron Fogel.** xxix, s. 7. April 23. Born Jan. 30, 1825. He belonged to the Dryland Lutheran Church. He was married twice : first to Eliza Bender, with whom he had two children, one of whom died; and later to Eliza Fehr, with whom he had three children, of whom one died. After having lived at Nazareth many years, moved to Pottsville, where he died.

945. **Lucinda Henrietta Clewell.** xxiv, n. 16. April 26. Daughter of Jacob and Rebecca (Seyfried) Clewell. Born May 14, 1830. During many years she was the teacher in the Infant Department of the Parochial School. She was also a member of the church choir, and a teacher in the Sunday-school. Died in Philadelphia.

946. **John Heller.** xxix, s. 8. May 19. Born in Palmer Township, Sept. 2, 1815. United with the Church at Schoeneck. In 1837 married Mary A. Seyfried, who died April 8, 1878. He had six children, three of whom died in infancy. In 1880 moved to Bethlehem, to the home of his daughter.

947. **John Henry Shive.** xxvii, s. 18. May 25. Infant son of William and Emma (Gramlich) Shive. Born and died in New York.

948. **Mary Louisa Clewell.** xxi, n. 15. May 25. Infant daughter of William Clewell.

949. **Mary Ellen Helm.** xxiv, n. 17. June 13. Daughter of Henry Helm. Born in Schuylkill Haven, April 11, 1863. Her mother died Oct. 30, 1869. Moved to Nazareth to her father. She was a faithful Christian.

950. **Amelia Christ.** m.n. Giersch. xxvi, n. 14. June 28. Daughter of Joseph Giersch. Born at Filetown, May 31, 1821. In her third year moved to Philadelphia, later to Niesky. Married the widower Richard Christ, Nov. 6, 1865.

951. **Beata Henry.** xxi, n. 16. Sept. 7. Infant daughter of Robert and Susie (Munger) Henry.

952. **Herman Eugene Etschman.** xxx, s. 1. Dec. 6. Son of Franklin and Jane (Neumeyer) Etschman. Born July 8, 1880.

1885.

953. **Mary Olivia Etschman.** xxi, n. 17. Jan. 1. Daughter of Franklin and Jane (Neumeyer) Etschman. Born Nov. 8, 1881.

954. **May Beitel.** xxi, n. 18. Jan. 23. Infant daughter of Lewis J. and Mary (Arnold) Beitel. Born at Easton, Oct. 28, 1884.

955. **Mary Turner,** m.n. Auman. xxvi, n. 15. March 11. Born Dec. 25, 1818, in Berks Co., Pa. Married James Turner, at Pottsville, Sept. 24, 1860. Moved to Nazareth in 1867, and soon after united with the Church.

956. **Dorothea Beck (Hessler),** m.n. Friebele. xxvi, n. 16. April 14. Born in Baden, May 1, 1810. Came to this country when in her nineteenth year. In Schoeneck married the widower, John Hessler, in 1830, and united with the Church. Removed to Hopedale, where her husband died in 1851. Four sons and four daughters, of whom one son and three daughters preceded her into eternity. Married the widower, Jacob Beck, March. 1856, who died the following year, very suddenly. In 1883, being feeble, she moved to Hazleton to her daughter, where she died.

957. **Beata Snyder.** xxvii, n. 1. May 4. Infant daughter of J. and M. L. Snyder.

958. **Caroline Elizabeth Ettwein.** xxix, n. 1. July 4. Daughter of John and Maria Ettwein, and great grand-daughter of Bishop John Ettwein. Born Jan. 23, 1822. Baptized and confirmed in the Lutheran Church, to which her parents belonged. Her father died May 20, 1848. In 1870 she united with the Moravian Church.

959. **Luella Eliza Beitel.** xxvii, n. 2. Sept. 24. Daughter of Richard O. and Emma (Boyer) Beitel. Born June 16, 1874.

1886.

960. **Josephine Klaus.** xxvi, n. 17. Jan. 4. Born in Baden, March 19, 1807. In 1866, after the death of her husband, she came to this country, living with her daughter, Mrs. A. Mattes. She belonged to the Roman Catholic Church. She had ten children, of whom six preceded her into eternity.

961. **Oliver Adam Cope.** xxix, s. 9. Jan. 28. Son of Jacob and Lavina Cope. Born March 26, 1859, in Salzburg Township. Baptized by the Rev. Joshua Jaeger. Confirmed in Nazareth, 1877. He lived here six years, learning his trade with his brother-in-law, Emanuel Venter. Married Sarah Jane Hoch, and then removed to Salzburg, hoping that a change of occupation, might aid in the restoration of his health. For five years he was an invalid. He had one son.

962. **Daniel G. Brown.** xxix, s. 10. June 12. Son of Charles and Christina (Heller) Brown. Born Aug. 16, 1832. Confirmed at the Forks Church. Married Lucinda S. Ebbecke. In 1864 moved to Nazareth, in 1885 to Ashland Station, becoming railroad agent there. United with the Moravian Church in 1864. During the last five years of his life a great sufferer. He had four children, three daughters and a son, of whom a daughter and the son preceded him to eternity.

963. **Lizzie Beitel.** xxvii, n. 3. June 24. Infant daughter of Lewis and Mary Beitel.

964. **Herbert Beitel.** xxx, s. 2. July 7. Infant son of Lewis and Mary Beitel.

965. **Maria Sybilla Clewell.** x, n. 18. July 24. Unmarried sister. Daughter of Christian and Maria (Kreiter) Clewell. Born at Niesky Feb. 13, 1801. Baptized by Brother Strohle, and confirmed at Schoeneck by Brother Theodore Shultz. She moved into the Sisters' House in 1829. In 1879 she moved into the home of Wm. Kern, remaining there until her end.

1887.

966. **Ann Eliza Fetter,** m.n. Horsfield. xxviii, n. 1. Jan. 3. Daughter of Timothy and Amy Horsfield. Born on Nantucket Island, Mass., July 13, 1804. After the death of her parents, when eleven years old, her grandmother Sarah

Horsfield, m.n. Mumford, took her to Bethlehem, where she attended the Young Ladies' Seminary, and was baptized by Brother Chas. F. Seidel. In her eighteenth year, she entered the Seminary as teacher. Married John George Fetter, Nov. 28, 1826, and moved to Lancaster, where she taught school. Her husband died Nov. 15, 1855. She then lived with her daughters at Lancaster and Bethlehem, and later at Nazareth, where she departed this life on Dec. 30. Aged 82 years.

967. **Nelson Ellwood Hertzog.** xxix, s. 11. Jan. 4. Son of William and Hermina Hertzog. Born at Fleetwood, Berks Co., Pa., Nov. 17, 1861. Married Amelia Leibengut, May 13, 1883. Died Dec. 29. He was not a member of this Church.

968. **Matilda Emilie Schneebeli.** xxix, n. 2. March 27. Daughter of Adolph and Louisa Fredericka Emilie Schneebeli. Born in Neusalz, Silesia, June 17, 1854. When in her eleventh year, she went to her aunt, Caroline Seidel, in Neudietendorf, Thuringia, with whom she lived several years, following her parents to this country in 1867. In 1873 confirmed in Nazareth. Died in Newark, N.J.

969. **Agnes Maria Kluge,** m.n. von Pannach. xxviii, n. 2. May 8. Born Nov. 8, 1807, near Kleinwelka, Saxony. Came to this country with her relative, the Rev. L. D. de Schweinitz, residing for some years in Salem, N.C., where she attended the Academy. Later, removed to Bethlehem, where she completed her education in the Young Ladies' Seminary, serving there as teacher until her marriage to the Rev. Charles F. Kluge, Sept. 9, 1828. With him she served in Lancaster, Linden Hall Seminary, New York, and in Nazareth Hall, of which her husband was principal, removing then to Salem, N.C. Her husband having been elected a member of the Unity's Elders' Conference, she moved to Berthelsdorf in 1853. Returned to this country after the General Synod of 1857, living in Bethlehem and Nazareth. After her husband's death, March 26, 1880, she removed to Bethlehem. Celebrated their golden wedding in 1878. She had five children, one daughter, who had been a teacher in Bethlehem Seminary twenty-seven years, preceding her into eternity. Departed this life unexpectedly, aged 79 years and 6 months.

970. **Beatus Miller.** xxx, s. 3. May 26.

971. **Maximilian Eugene Grunert.** xxix, s. 12. June 4. Presbyter of the Church. Born in Niesky, Prussia, Feb. 26, 1823. He was educated in the College and Theological Seminary of the German Province, and after serving in several educational institutions in Germany, came to this country in 1851, entering the service in the Southern Province where he was pastor in Bethania and Principal of the Salem Academy and also a member of the Provincial Board. In 1877 he accepted the appointment as pastor of the church at Emmaus, Pa., and in 1879 became resident professor in the Theological Seminary at Bethlehem. During the winter of 1882-83 he filled the pulpit of the church at Nazareth, with great faithfulness, there being no pastor here at that time. On account of failing health, he retired to Nazareth, in 1886. He was a very gifted man, an excellent preacher, a faithful servant of the Lord and an humble and loving follower of the Saviour. He was married three times. Died very suddenly, aged 64 years. Two sons and two daughters survived him.

972. **Martha Woodring Christ.** xxvii, n. 4. Nov. 7. Daughter of Francis and
Aquilla Christ. Born March 30, 1882.

973. **Amelia Eliza Clewell (Grunewald)**, m.n. Bardill. xxviii, n. 3. Nov. 7.
Daughter of George R. and Catharine (Schneider) Bardill. Born Sept. 9,
1814. Married Theodore Ferdinand Grunewald, Oct. 6, 1836, who died
Aug. 9, 1848. She had two children, one of whom died in infancy. Married
the widower, Jacob Clewell, Sr., Oct. 11, 1864. He died Jan. 30, 1871.

974. **Raymond Eugene Ziegler.** xxx, s. 4. Nov. 18. Infant son of Max and
Alice Ziegler. Born Aug. 17, 1886.

975. **Beatus Beil.** xxx, s. 5. Dec. 7. Infant son of M. W. and Jane (Gruver) Beil.

976. **Comenius Senseman.** xxix, s. 13. Dec. 4. Son of Christian David and
Anna Eliza (Ritter) Senseman. Born Sept. 10, 1818, in Nazareth. Married,
in Bethlehem, May, 1847, Sophia Henrietta Reichel, who departed this life,
Dec. 28, 1872. For more than forty years he conducted the store which his
father and elder brother had had. He spent his entire life in the house in
which he had been born. His marriage was blessed with two children, a son
and daughter, the former dying in his infancy. Married Caroline Knauss,
m.n. Dizinger, widow of the Rev. F. W. Knauss, July 11, 1876. An accident,
by which one of his limbs was fractured, hastened his end.

977. **Charles Samuel O'Neill.** xxx, s. 6. Dec. 21. Infant son of William and
Hattie (Venter) O'Neill. Born Nazareth, July 24, 1887. Died in Philadelphia, where the parents reside.

1888.

978. **Irwin Eugene Beitel.** xxx, s. 7. Feb. 1. Infant son of Lewis and Mary
(Arnold) Beitel.

979. **Edmund Ricksecker.** xxix, s. 14. April 19. Son of George and Anna
Elizabeth (Beitel) Ricksecker. Born in Nazareth, Oct. 6, 1814. Baptized
by Brother Meder, Oct. 9, 1814, and confirmed by Brother W. H. Van Vleck,
April 12, 1829. Married Olivia Miksch, March 12, 1840. He had two sons
and two daughters, one son dying in his childhood. After having followed
his trade as watchmaker for some years, he engaged in the nursery business,
in which he was very successful. Together with several others, he endeavored
to beautify and improve the graveyard, planting a great variety of trees and
shrubbery, succeeding well. He was Justice of the Peace and Surveyor. In
the Church, as well as in the community, he was a prominent and greatly
respected man, possessed of unusual ability. Modest and retiring, he was a
very worthy member of the Church and an humble, consistent Christian. In
the Church he filled various offices, having been a sacristan for many years, a
member of the trombone choir, assisting in the orchestra of the choir, an Elder
and member of the Parochial School Board, and Treasurer of the Church.
He died very suddenly of heart disease, aged 73 years.

980. **George Knauss.** xxix, s. 15. May 14. Son of Samuel and Maria (Dengler)
Knauss. Born in Colebrookdale, Bucks County, Pa., Oct. 28, 1812. Baptized and confirmed in the Reformed Church, to which he belonged to his
death. Removed to Nazareth about forty years ago, working at his trade as
tanner here and in the neighborhood. Married Annabella Beitel, daughter
of John Beitel, July 27, 1845. He had one son, William V. Knauss, of
Bethlehem.

981. **Beata Christ.** xxvii, n. 5. June 26.

982. **Mary Eva Kingkinger,** m.n. Snyder. xxviii, n. 4. Oct. 14. Daughter of William and Margaret Snyder. Born in Harmony, Warren County, N.J., June 8, 1831. Baptized and confirmed in the Lutheran Church. Married Horace F. Kingkinger, Aug. 22, 1852. Moved to Nazareth in 1858. United with the Moravian Church in 1877. She had four children, one daughter and three sons, all of whom survive.

983. **Christian Frederick Martin, Jr.** xxix, s. 16. Nov. 15. Son of Christian Frederick and Lucia Ottilia (Kuehle) Martin. Born in Vienna, Austria, Oct. 2, 1825, and baptized two days later. When three years old, removed, with his parents, to Neukirchen, Saxony, the birthplace of his father. In his seventh year, came with his parents to the United States, residing five years in New York; then to Cherry Hill, where his father established the business of guitar making. Confirmed at Schoeneck by Brother Edward Rondthaler, Sr. Married Anna Maria Alleman, May 24, 1849. She died Feb. 23, 1861. This union was blessed with three children, two daughters and a son, of whom one daughter survived. Married Lucinda Leibfried, March 18, 1862. He had four daughters and a son, all of whom survived. Although afflicted in his youth with a severe nervous affection, he recovered, enjoying good health until a short time before his death, and was able to carry on the extensive business founded by his father. He was a prominent and influential citizen, and served as chief burgess, and was a member of town council. He was an active member of the Church, serving as trustee, respected and beloved.

984. **John Neumeyer.** xxix, s. 17. Dec. 14. Son of Theobald and Elizabeth Neumeyer. Born in Kerzenheim, Rhenish Bavaria, Oct. 29, 1813. After having learned his trade as blacksmith, with his father, he came to this country when in his twenty-third year, and settled in Bethlehem. Here he married Caroline Schultz, daughter of Samuel Schultz, Dec. 6, 1840. In 1843 moved to Christianspring, where he continued to live thirty-seven years, moving to Nazareth in 1880. He had thirteen children, all of whom, with the exception of one, who died in childhood, survived their father. He had thirty-four grand-children, three of whom have died.

1889.

985. **William DeReamer.** xxix, s. 18. Jan. 9. Son of John DeReamer, born in Warren Co., N.J., Nov. 16, 1825. Married Mary Ann Ely, of Rosscommon, Pa., Oct. 28, 1854. Baptized March 21, 1877, in the Moravian Church at Nazareth. He had two sons and two daughters.

986. **Helen May Heintzelman.** xxvii, n. 6. Feb. 10. Infant daughter of Francis and Hannah Heintzelman. Born Aug. 8, 1888.

987. **Beatus Neumeyer.** xxx, s. 8. May 30. Infant son of Morris and Eva G. Neumeyer.

988. **James Monroe Kingkinger.** xxxi, s. 1. July 12. Son of Horace F. and Mary E. Kingkinger. Born Dec. 29, 1852. Baptized and confirmed in the Lutheran Church. Not a member of the Moravian Church.

989. **Conrad Kichline.** xxxii, s. 1. Aug. 31. Son of Andrew and Catharine (Rau) Kichline. Born in Hanover Township, May 7, 1810. Confirmed in Lutheran Church, but united with the Moravian Church many years ago·

Married Eloisa Sachsen, of Emmaus, Feb. 14, 1836, who died April 18, 1857. He had a son and three daughters, all of whom died before their father. Married the widow, Sarah Gruver, May 13, 1858. For many years he was superintendent of the graveyard and grave-digger, doing much to beautify the grounds, in which he took great pride. He was also Poor Director of the County. He suffered greatly during his last illness.

990. **Annie Amanda Jane Hoffeditz.** xxix, n. 3. Oct. 12. Youngest daughter of William and Eva (Nieth) Hoffeditz. Born at Nazareth, May 30, 1874.

991. **Edward Theodore Grunewald.** xxxii, s. 2. Dec. 7. Son of Theodore Ferdinand and Amelia (Bardill) Grunewald. Born Sept. 27, 1837. His father died when he was in his eleventh year. Married Julia Weaver, daughter of Jacob Weaver, Sept. 29, 1859, who died July 25, 1875. One daughter, who died in infancy. Married Amelia Etschman, May 13, 1880. During about two years he was secretary and treasurer of the Congregation. For many years an officer of the Moravian Historical Society; a member of the Parochial School Board; Librarian of the Sunday-school; one of the Sacristans of the church; Secretary of the Agricultural Society; and Borough Treasurer. Also Jury Commissioner and Justice of the Peace. He also represented the Congregation at several Synods and Conferences. A very useful man and good citizen and member of the Church. Died very suddenly of neuralgia of the heart.

1890.

992. **Charlotte Elizabeth Reichel,** m.n. Meas. xxviii, n. 5. Jan. 9. Daughter of Thomas Meas. Born Sept. 21, 1820. Confirmed in Bethlehem in 1836. Educated in Bethlehem Seminary, where she also was engaged as teacher of music. Married the Rev. Edward H. Reichel, (appointed pastor of the Church in Camden Valley, N.Y.,) March 22, 1849. In 1854 moved to Nazareth, her husband having been appointed principal of Nazareth Hall. For twelve years she faithfully discharged her duties in this position. In 1866 her husband retired, on account of impaired health. A son died in 1874, and her husband, suddenly, Sept. 7, 1877. She died very unexpectedly in Brooklyn, while on a visit to her daughter. Three children, two sons and a daughter, one of the sons preceding his mother into eternity.

993. **Harriet Cecilia Bates,** m.n. Danke. xxviii, n. 6. Jan. 16. Daughter of John Frederick and Barbara Danke. Born in Nazareth, Dec. 16, 1820. Married Harvey Bates, Sept. 1, 1844. She then moved to Wilkes-Barre. Her husband died in 1873. She had seven children, of whom two daughters have departed this life. After the death of her husband, returned to Schoeneck to her brother, Alfred Danke. She was a very faithful, earnest Christian.

994. **Beata Etschman.** xxvii, n. 7. Jan. 28. Infant daughter of Edwin and Mary Etschman.

995. **Harry P. B. Long.** xxxii, s. 3. April 15. Son of Samuel and Mary Long. Born Aug. 7, 1856, at New Castle, Pa. Married Lizzie Willower, at Creston, Ohio. Moved to Philadelphia in 1888. He was a member of the Methodist Episcopal Church.

996. **Walter Franklin Shive.** xxx, s. 9. May 25.

997. **Henry Klein.** xxxii, s. 4. June 13. Born in Gundersweiler, Bavarian Palatinate, Sept. 11, 1825. Having taken part in the democratic uprising of

1848, he was compelled to emigrate to America in 1850. Married Agnes Lutz, May 6, 1855, in New York. Came to Nazareth and united with the Church in 1860. Served in the army from 1862 to 1863.

998. **Francis Benjamin Heintzelman.** xxxii, s. 5. Aug. 11. Son of Jacob and Mary Heintzelman. Born Feb. 13, 1859. Married Hannah Spengler, Feb. 28, 1882. Died in Pen Argyl, where he was temporarily employed. He had a son and daughter, the latter dying in infancy.

999. **William Richard Beitel.** xxx, s. 10. Sept. 24. Son of John Frederick and Ida E. (Miksch) Beitel. Born July 27, 1885.

1000. **Lottie Olivia Walter.** xxvii, n. 8. Oct. 2. Infant daughter of Alfred and Sabina (Siegfried) Walter. Born Aug. 13, 1890.

1001. **Francis Jordan.** xxxii, s. 6. Died Aug. 13, 1885. Re-interred here Oct. 15, 1890. Born in Philadelphia, June 26, 1815. Died at Ocean Beach, N.J., Aug. 13, 1885, aged seventy years, one month and eighteen days. He was the youngest son of John and Elizabeth (Henry) Jordan, his grandfather, William Henry, having long been a member of the Church at Nazareth. Married Emily Woolf, Dec. 10, 1839. He had thirteen children, of whom nine survived. United with the Moravian Church in Philadelphia, in 1850. For nearly twenty years served as Treasurer of the congregation and was a member of the Board of Elders. He represented the congregation at seven synods, and was elected as a delegate to the General Synod of 1869, but was unable to attend. He was buried in Woodland Cemetery; but his remains were removed to Nazareth in 1890.

1002. **Emily Jordan,** m.n. Woolf. xxviii, n. 7. Sept. 4, 1889. Re-interred here Oct. 15, 1890. Daughter of John L. and Margaret (Ewing) Woolf, and widow of Francis Jordan. Born in Philadelphia, Nov. 12, 1821. Married to Francis Jordan, Dec. 10, 1839. United with the Moravian Church in Philadelphia in 1842. Died in Nazareth, Sept. 4, 1889, aged 67 years, 9 months and 23 days. She was buried in Woodland Cemetery, but removed to Nazareth in 1890.

1003· **Lydia Beitel,** m.n. Bauer. xxviii, n. 8. Oct. 23. Daughter of Johann Gottlieb and Anna Maria (Romig) Bauer. Born in Bushkill Township, April 15, 1806. In Sept., 1833, moved to Nazareth, with her widowed mother. Married Philip Hasselberger Dec. 31, 1845, who died May 3, 1846. Married the widower John Beitel, Oct. 11, 1850, who died Aug. 1, 1870. She was an invalid during many years.

1004. **Alfred Raymond Beitel.** xxx, s. 11. Oct. 26. Infant son of Lewis and Mary (Arnold) Beitel. Born in Newark, N.J., July 8, 1890. The sixth child buried here by the parents.

1891.

1005. **Beata Ziegler.** xxvii, n. 9. Feb. 4. Infant daughter of Herman and Sarah (Smith) Ziegler.

1006. **May Christina Etschman.** xxvii, n. 10. June 9. Infant daughter of Franklin and Jane (Neumeyer) Etschman. Born Feb. 16, 1890.

1007. **Frank Levin Frack.** xxx, s. 12. Sept. 21. Infant son of Edward and Annie (Seyfried) Frack. Born Dec. 18, 1890.

1008. **Walter Edwin Steininger.** xxx, s. 13. Sept. 27. Infant son of Enos and Stella (Beisel) Steininger. Born April 9, 1891.

1009. **Eliza Ann Fogel,** m.n. Fehr. xxviii, n. 9. Oct. 21. Born at Boulton, Oct. 23, 1829. Married Aaron Fogel. Died in Philadelphia. Not a member of the Church.

1010. **Mary Elizabeth Kiefer.** xxix, n. 4. Nov. 20. Daughter of William R. and Mary (Heller) Kiefer. Born in Nazareth, July 3, 1873.

1011. **Jemima Kreider,** m.n. Leinbach. xxviii, n. 10. Dec. 15. Daughter of Joseph and Christina (Christ) Leinbach. Born in Emmaus, Feb. 9, 1808. When an infant, her parents removed to Lancaster, where she was confirmed. Married the widower Daniel Kreider, Nov. 27, 1853, who died at Lititz, Jan. 3, 1868. Then she moved to Lancaster and in 1890 to Nazareth, with the family of her stepson, William E. Kreider.

1012. **Araminta Emilie Wenhold,** m.n. Brunner. xxviii, n. 11. Dec. 30. Daughter of John Jacob and Maria Salome (Beitel) Brunner. Born in Nazareth, Dec. 23, 1813. Married Charles Wenhold, Nov. 26, 1837.

1892.

1013. **Sophia Catharine Ettwein,** m.n. Miksch. xxviii, n. 12. Jan. 17. Daughter of Jacob and Catharine (Weinland) Miksch. Born July 15, 1831. Married Jacob Ettwein, April 11, 1854. She had two daughters, who died in their infancy.

1014. **Sarah Kichline,** m.n. Hartman. xxviii, n. 13. Jan. 22. Daughter of Abraham and Catharine (Beisel) Hartman. Born in Allen Township, Feb. 13, 1817. Baptized and confirmed in the Lutheran Church. Married George Gruver, Jan. 1, 1838. She had one son and two daughters. Her husband died April 25, 1854. Married the widower Conrad Kichline, May 13, 1858. Later united with the Moravian Church. Her second husband died Aug. 31, 1889. Three children, seventeen grandchildren, and twenty-three great grandchildren survived her.

1015. **Frank E. Schulin.** xxxi, s. 2. Feb. 11. Born in Gnadenberg, Prussia, Feb. 13, 1859. He was a member of the First Church in New York, and a trustee of the Congregation. At his particular request, his pastor, the Rev. E. T. Kluge, brought his remains to Nazareth for interment in a Moravian graveyard with Moravian ceremonies.

1016. **Arthur James Kern.** xxx, s. 14. Feb. 24. Infant son of Julius and Catharine (Oplinger) Kern. Born Feb. 16, 1892.

1017. **Sarah Kern,** m.n. Lichtenthaeler. xxviii, n. 14. Feb. 26. Eldest daughter of Adolph and Elizabeth (Knauss) Lichtenthaeler. Born in Lititz, Nov. 8, 1803. Baptized the next day (according to the old custom) by Bishop Herbst. She was educated in Linden Hall Seminary. Confirmed by Bishop Benade, Aug. 13, 1818. In 1820 entered Linden Hall Seminary as teacher, serving for thirteen years, when she was called to be the spiritual laboress of the Single Sisters in Bethlehem. In 1837, Oct. 17, she married the widower, Andrew G. Kern, of Nazareth. She had two sons and two daughters. Three children and seventeen grand-children survived her. Her husband died December 25, 1874. She was generally respected and loved.

1018. **John Neumeyer Wunderly.** xxx, s. 15. March 13. Son of Frank and Caroline (Neumeyer) Wunderly. Born Sept. 19, 1891.

1019. **Rebecca Roberts**, m.n. Baker. xxviii, n. 15. March 31. Born in Oswego, N.Y., March 3, 1833. Married in 1870 to Smith Knight, and in 1875 to William Roberts. She did not belong to the Church.

1020. **Eudora Bardill**, m.n. Kreidler. xxviii, n. 16. April 17. Daughter of John and Julianna (Kramer) Kreidler. Born in Bethlehem Township, Sept. 20, 1863. Baptized and confirmed in the Lutheran Church. In her fourteenth year moved to Nazareth, to her uncle, Samuel R. Odenwelder. United with the Moravian Church in 1891. Married John F. Bardill, April 2, 1891. A son survived her.

1021. **Elizabeth Christ**, m.n. Daniel. xxviii, n. 17. May 5. Youngest daughter of Adam and Catharine (Wagoner) Daniel. Born in Lower Nazareth Township, Oct. 6, 1823. Baptized and confirmed in Lutheran Church. Attended Parochial School at Nazareth and private school of Brother F. F. Hagen. She aided in organizing the first Sunday-school in Nazareth. After teaching at Christianspring, entered Linden Hall Seminary as teacher. While at Lititz, assisted in organizing the Sunday-school at that place. In 1849 returned home, her mother being in feeble health, and dying in 1850. Married William Christ, Nov. 24, 1853, and moved to Nazareth, and soon after united with the Church. On account of a mental affliction was removed to the Norristown Asylum in 1892, where she departed this life, aged sixty-eight years. One daughter survived her.

1022. **James William Christ**. xxxii, s. 7. May 27. Son of John Jacob and Anna Justina (Knauss) Christ. Born in Nazareth, May 11, 1809. Educated in Nazareth Hall. Married Elizabeth Daniel, Nov. 24, 1853. Served as Trustee of the congregation and as a member of the Parochial School Board. He was long one of the principal officers of the Water Company. He was a man of more than ordinary intelligence, and was much respected by all. Three weeks after the sad death of his wife, he departed this life, aged 83 years.

1023. **Elizabeth Catharine Long**, m.n. Willower. xxx, n. 1. Aug. 20. Daughter of Daniel and Maria (Lind) Willower. Born in South Easton, July 25, 1860. Married Ed. R. Post, Sept. 11, 1879, living in Medina, Ohio, from whom she was separated. Married Harry Long at Creston, Ohio, Jan. 1, 1887, moving to Philadelphia in 1888, where he died, April 15, 1890. She was a member of the Baptist Church. While on a visit to her mother, at that time living in Ohio, she died.

1024. **Abraham Lichtenthaeler**. xxxii, s. 8. Oct. 2. Son of Adolph and Elizabeth (Knauss) Lichtenthaeler. Born in Lititz, April 15, 1818. Married Charlotte Kreider, daughter of Samuel and Elizabeth Kreider, Oct. 26, 1843. Having been called to mission-service, he was ordained by Bishop Benade in November, 1843, and sailed for Jamaica, where he served in a number of congregations. He made many trying experiences, especially during the prevalence of the cholera in Jamaica, and later the small-pox. In 1859 he was called to New Carmel. During his ministry here, the great revival took place. In 1864 he was appointed Superintendent of the Jamaica mission. In 1866 he was ordained Presbyter by Bishop Westerby. In 1869, attended the General Synod in Herrnhut. In 1873 he was appointed Superintendent of the Mission in St. Kitts, and in 1875 of St. Thomas. In 1877 he was obliged to retire from active service, on account of his health, and moved to Nazareth. Two children preceded him to eternity, and two sons and four daughters survived him.

1893.

1025. **Elizabeth Shoemaker Reeves.** xxvii, n. 11. Jan. 28. Daughter of the late Charles Reeves and his wife Flora, m.n. Rominger. Born in Philadelphia, Oct. 20, 1882. Entered Linden Hall Seminary, in Jan., 1890, where she died of diphtheria, Jan. 28, 1893. Remains brought to Nazareth for interment.

1026. **Lillian Ellen Becker.** xxix, n. 5. March 10. Daughter of Dr. Aaron and Caroline (Fetter) Becker. Born in Bethlehem, April 30, 1858. She was afflicted with epilepsy from her childhood, and died here rather suddenly, when on a visit to her relatives, Brother and Sister Lennert.

1027. **George Frederick Kreider.** xxxi, s. 3. Re-interred March 25. Son of William and Josephine (Demuth) Kreider. Born in Lititz, April 18, 1856. Confirmed in Lancaster in 1873; died in Lancaster, May 7, 1875.

1028. **Clara Phillips,** m. n. Klingman. xxx, n. 2. April 25. Wife of Samuel J. Phillips, and daughter of William and Mary (Ott) Klingman. Born in Bangor, Pa., Dec. 24, 1856. Married Samuel Phillips, May 19, 1873. Died in Washington, D. C., and at her special request, was buried here. Two daughters survived her.

1029. **Laura Schmickly,** m.n. Ricksecker. xxx, n. 3. April 28. Daughter of Lucius and Sabina (Weaver) Ricksecker. Born in Nazareth, March 11, 1867. Confirmed here in 1884. Married Milton H. Schmickly, July 14, 1891. A week after the birth of a son, departed this life at Easton.

1030. **Edwin S. Kortz.** xxxii, s. 9. May 10. Son of Reuben and Isabella Traill Kortz; born in Easton, Sept. 28, 1855. Lived in New York and Philadelphia, being confirmed in the Moravian Church in the latter city, later being a member of the Board of Trustees and Elders. Married Jane Kern, Dec. 6, 1882. Died in Philadelphia. A son and daughter survive.

1031. **William Lawrence Lennert.** xxxii, s. 10. June 21. For many years pastor of the church at Nazareth; son of John Peter and Johanna (Knauss) Lennert; born in Lititz, April 5, 1812. Educated at Nazareth Hall and the Theological Seminary. Entered Nazareth Hall as teacher in 1832, continuing until 1836. He had offered his services to the Mission Board, but was needed in the home service and continued here. Married Maria Caroline Schmidt, daughter of Dr. H. Schmidt, Dec. 9, 1836, and was ordained as Deacon by Bishop Benade, having been called as pastor to York, Pa., where he labored successfully ten years. Ordained Presbyter by Bishop Peter Wolle, May 23, 1847, and called as pastor to Hebron, (Lebanon County,) Pa. During his pastorate the church in Lebanon was built. In 1849 called to Nazareth, continuing here until 1860. His wife died Nov. 5, 1856. Married Suzette Fetter, Feb. 4, 1858. In 1860 he was appointed pastor at Lebanon, for the second time. In 1866 pastor at Hope, Ind., and in 1870 at New Dorp, Staten Island. After serving the Church forty years, he was obliged, by failing health, to retire in 1876. A son by his first marriage survived. He was a faithful man, endeared to all by his genial and affectionate manner.

1032. **Verena May DeReamer.** xxvii, n. 12. Sept. 2. Infant daughter of Thomas and Antoinette (Kirchenthal) DeReamer. Born Jan. 13, 1893.

1033. **Charles Kotz.** xxxii, s. 11. Oct. 2. Son of Jacob and Elizabeth (Frankenfield) Kotz. Born May 14, 1824, in Williams Township, Northampton County, Pa. Married Sarah Louisa Stoudt, Jan. 5, 1854. Confirmed in Moravian Church at Nazareth in 1860.

1034. **Catharine Wietsche,** m.n. Hilberg. xxx, n. 4. Oct. 20. Daughter of Jonas and Anna Hilberg. Born in Raffel, Hesse, Germany, May 1, 1817 When fifteen years old came to this country, and soon after her arrival came to Nazareth. Married Carl Wietsche, Dec. 8, 1855, and in 1857, she and her husband united with the Church. They had two sons who died in their childhood. Her husband died April 5, 1868. Being in feeble health, she went to Kreidlersville to her niece, where she died.

1035. **Caroline Louisa Sellers,** m.n. Bardill. xxx, n. 5. Dec. 8. Daughter of George Rudolph and Catharine (Schneider) Bardill. Born Feb. 25, 1819. Married Dr. Charles Sellers, May 21, 1840, who died Sept. 13, 1883. She had two daughters, who have survived their mother. For twenty-five years she served the Church as *Dienerin*. While on a visit to her daughter in Bethlehem, she died, aged 74 years.

1894.

1036. **Lucile DeReamer.** xxvii, n. 13. March 10. Daughter of Clinton and Jennie (Pohl) DeReamer. Born in Easton, June 22, 1893. Died in Philadelphia.

1037. **Elizabeth Ottilia Shive.** xxix, n. 6. March 18. Daughter of William and Emma (Gramlich) Shive. Born Sept. 7, 1877. While attending the instruction preparatory to confirmation, she was taken ill, and died on Palm Sunday, aged 16 years.

1038. **Elizabeth Miksch,** m.n. Clewell. xxx, n. 6. May 19. Daughter of George and Johanna (Knauss) Clewell; born in Schoeneck, Feb. 2, 1799. Her father died March 17, 1816, and April 23, 1817 she entered the Nazareth Sisters' House. Married Joseph Miksch April 11, 1820, and moved to Bethlehem. She had two daughters, Olivia, widow of Edmund Ricksecker, and Angelica, wife of Nathaniel Wolle, of Lititz, both of whom survived their mother. Her husband died Aug. 17, 1824, and she then returned to Nazareth, after the marriage of her youngest daughter, making her home with the elder one, Mrs. Ricksecker. Although attaining so great an age, she was seldom ill; always cheerful and trustful, but during the last years often longing for her eternal home. She was survived by two children, six grand-children, fourteen great-grand-children, and four great-great-grand-children. She was the oldest member of the congregation and the oldest inhabitant of Nazareth. Aged 95 years, 3 months and 17 days.

1039. **Louisa Fredericka Emilie Schneebeli,** m.n. Engler. xxx, n. 7. Aug. 4. Daughter of Christoph and Louisa Engler; born in Neudietendorf, Germany, June 27, 1831. For a number of years she was in charge of the school for small children. Married Adolph Schneebeli, July 13, 1852, living then in Neusalz, Silesia, twelve years. Then they emigrated to this country; residing in Bethlehem from 1864–66, when they moved to Nazareth. Six children survive.

1040. **John Webb.** xxxi, s. 4. Aug. 15. Son of Thomas Webb, of Christiana Jamaica, West Indies. Born May 1, 1876, in Kansas. His mother died in June, 1894. He was a pupil of Nazareth Hall, preparing to enter the Moravian College and Theological Seminary in Bethlehem. He was drowned at Saylor's Lake, while vainly trying to rescue a companion, Edward Townsend.

1041. **Susan Elizabeth Giering,** m.n. Saylor. xxx, n. 8. Sept. 1. Daughter of Frederick and Sarah (Fehr) Saylor. Born in Bushkill Township, Sept. 3, 1830. Married Florian F. Giering, of Emmaus, Feb. 28, 1850. Lived in Catasauqua for nineteen years. In 1872 moved to Bethlehem, where she united with the Moravian Church. In 1875 removed to Nazareth. Six children survived.

1042. **Charles Francis Whitesell.** xxxii, s. 12. Dec. 25. Son of Benjamin and Catharine (Leibert) Whitesell. Born in Newark, N.J., June 2, 1839. After the death of his father (who lost his life in a railroad accident in 1841), he lived in the family of Andrew Whitesell in Nazareth. He was confirmed in the Lutheran Church at Dryland. Married Emmaline Hahn, Jan. 26, 1867. Lived in Washington, D.C., seven years. In 1876 came to Schoeneck and united with that congregation.

1895.

1043. **Caroline Neumeyer,** m.n. Schultz. xxx, n. 9. Feb. 3. Daughter of Samuel Schultz and his wife, m.n. Peissert. Born in Bethlehem, June 3, 1823. Married John Neumeyer, Dec. 6, 1840. After living near Bethlehem for some time, moved to Christianspring in 1843, where they resided thirty-seven years, moving to Nazareth in 1880. Her husband died Dec. 14, 1888. Thirteen children, eleven of whom survive. She had forty-two grand-children (of whom six died), and five great-grand-children.

1044. **Jacob Heintzelman.** xxxii, s. 13. Feb. 7. Son of John and Regina Heintzelman. Born in Marbach, Würtemberg, Nov. 7, 1830. Baptized and confirmed in the Catholic Church. In 1856 came to America and settled in Nazareth, where he married Mary Roesch, June 1, 1857. United with the Moravian Church in 1860. Four children survive.

1045. **Sophia Theresa Bardill,** m.n. Milchsack. xxx, n. 10. Feb. 18. Daughter of Augustus and Hannah (Everett) Milchsack. Born in Bethlehem, June 28, 1832. Married J. Henry Bardill, April 18, 1854. A son and daughter survive.

1046. **Maria Sophia Beitel,** m.n. Kern. xxx, n. 11. March 26. Daughter of John Christian and Maria Elizabeth (Bishop) Kern. Born in Bethlehem, June 24, 1814. Married Josiah O. Beitel, Oct. 1, 1833, their married life extending over a period of more than sixty-one years. She had five sons, all of whom survive. She had nineteen grand-children and six great grand-children.

1047. **Elizabeth Michael,** m.n. Moore. xxx, n. 12. April 6. Born in Lehigh County, Pa., Oct. 5, 1809. Married Gotthold Benjamin Michael in 1828. After having lived a few years in Easton, returned to Nazareth. Her husband died Dec. 4, 1863. She had seven children, four of whom survived their mother. She had twelve grand-children, and three great grand-children.

1048. **Augustus H. Montgomery.** xxxii, s. 14. June 27. Son of Francis W. and Sarah Montgomery. Born in Auburn, Maine, Aug. 5, 1856. Not a member of the Moravian Church.

1049. **James Leibert.** xxxi, s. 5. July 4. Son of the Rev. Eugene and Sarah (Zorn) Leibert. Born at New Dorp, Staten Island, Sept. 23, 1863. Moved to Nazareth in 1867, when his father was appointed Principal of Nazareth Hall. Educated in the Hall and the Theological Seminary. Entered Nazareth Hall as teacher in 1884, serving there until 1892, when his father retired from the principalship. Entered the Correspondence School of Mining and Engineering in Scranton. In Jan., 1894, returned to the home of his parents, being in poor health. He was an excellent teacher, and was a prominent member of the church choir.

1050. **Christian Musselman.** xxxii, s. 15. July 13. Son of David and Anna Barbara (Roth) Musselman; born at Christianspring, Dec. 3, 1809. Baptized and confirmed in the Lutheran Church. In 1833 united with the Moravian Church at Nazareth. Married Sarah Zimmerman, of Philadelphia, April 24, 1839. Two children, both dying in infancy. His wife died Jan. 15, 1880. For many years he served as one of the sacristans (dieners), as a trustee for upwards of eight years, and as elder for more than eleven years. He was also chief burgess of Nazareth seven years. Since the death of his wife, he had lived with Dr. and Mrs. P. Walter.

1051. **William Eugene Kreider.** xxxii, s. 16. Aug. 29. Son of Daniel and Mary Louisa (Lennert) Kreider. Born in Lititz, May 8, 1828. Educated in Brother J. Beck's School. For sixteen years he was a member of the Lititz trombone choir. Married Josephine Demuth, of Lancaster, Aug. 30, 1855. In 1865 moved to Lancaster, where he held various offices in the church. He was engaged in the Prothonotary's Office for twenty-four years. His health being impaired, he moved to Nazareth in June, 1890. He is survived by a daughter and a son, the Rev. Charles Kreider, Principal of Linden Hall Seminary.

1052. **John Henry Ritter.** xxxii, s. 17. Sept. 19. Son of Charles and Catharine (Schneider) Ritter. Born in Lower Nazareth Township, Aug. 29, 1838. Baptized and confirmed in the Lutheran Church. Married Louisa Magdalene Culver. He had one son, who survived him. United with the Moravian Church in 1877.

1053. **James Daniel.** xxxii, s. 18. Oct. 9. Son of Abraham and Mary Ann Daniel. Born in Moore Township, Oct. 4, 1831. Baptized and confirmed in the Lutheran Church. Married Mary Ann Schmidt, March 12, 1854. In 1857 he united with the Moravian Church. For eight years he was Superintendent of the graveyard and grave-digger. For some years he and his wife were kindly cared for by the King's Daughters and friends, but finally, as both were poor and helpless, they were taken to the Almshouse, where both died.

1054. **Grace Eliza Beil.** xxvii, n. 14. Nov. 4. Infant daughter of Myron W. and Mary Jane (Gruver) Beil. Born July 15, 1895.

1055. **Frederick William Haas.** xxxi, s. 6. Nov. 7. Son of Robert and Elizabeth (Lind) Haas. Born in Nazareth, April 10, 1873. Confirmed in 1888. United with the First Moravian Church in Philadelphia, in 1892. Graduated from the Philadelphia College of Pharmacy, April 19, 1894, and secured a position in Pittsburgh. There he united with the Reformed Church in 1895. During the summer he accompanied his father on a European tour. Died of typhoid fever in an Alleghany City Hospital, three hours after his parents and brother had arrived. He was an unusually bright young man, greatly beloved, and a faithful Christian.

1056. **Seward Allen Streepy.** xxxi, s. 7. Dec. 24. Son of John and Seraphine (Statler) Streepy. Born Sept. 22, 1860. He worked in Belvidere and Easton and finally here. Confirmed April 14, 1878. He was in failing health during several years.

1896.

1057. **Henry Helm.** xxxiii, s. 2. Jan. 8. Son of John and Catharine Helm; born in Hanover Township, Lebanon County, Pa., Dec. 7, 1828. Prior to his removal to Nazareth, he had lived in Schuylkill Haven and Shamokin, where he belonged to the Evangelical Church. Married Abia Kiehner, with whom he had four sons and two daughters, both daughters and two sons having died before their father. His wife died Oct. 30, 1869. He married the widow of the late William Beitel, Eliza Ann (Ruch) Beitel, Jan. 15, 1878, since which time he resided here, uniting with the Moravian Church, June, 1878. He was a faithful member and devout Christian.

1058. **John David Loux.** xxxi, s. 8. Jan. 19. Son of Ephraim and Sabina (Trein) Loux; born in Aluta, Pa., Jan. 9, 1875. Baptized and confirmed in the Schoeneck church. He was an active member of the C. E. Society, and of the Sunday-school, and a very pious young man.

1059. **Louis Ferdinand Schneebeli.** xxx, s. 16. Feb. 16. Son of G. A. and Carrie (Schneider) Schneebeli. Born May 13, 1891.

1060. **Maria Magdalene Demuth,** m.n. Keller. xxxi, n. 1. April 6. Daughter of Andrew and Maria Keller. Born in Lancaster, Nov. 26, 1810. Baptized and confirmed in the Lutheran Church; but after her marriage to William Demuth, Sept. 4, 1828, united with the Moravian Church. She had seven children; one son and six daughters. Her husband died in Aug., 1870. After spending eighty years in Lancaster, removed to Nazareth in 1890, with her daughter.

1061. **Eliza Ann Helm,** m.n. Ruch (Beitel). xxxi, n. 2. May 2. Daughter of Peter Ruch. Born in Allen Township, Northampton County, Pa., July 6, 1818; baptized and confirmed in the Dryland Church. Her parents died when she was five years old, and soon after she came to Nazareth. Married William Beitel, Nov. 26, 1837, and united with the Moravian Church shortly afterwards. Her husband died, Aug. 26, 1869. She had four children, three sons and a daughter, of whom a son survived her. Married the widower, Henry Helm, Jan. 15, 1878. He died Jan. 8, 1896. During the last years of her life she had been an invalid.

1062. **Francisca Mattes,** m.n. Birsner. xxxi, n. 3. May 15. Born in Biesendorf, Baden, Germany, Jan. 12, 1835. Baptized and confirmed in the Catholic Church. Came to United States in 1854, and settled in Easton. Married Anton Mattes, Feb. 18, 1855. Moved to Nazareth in 1859, and in 1862 united with the Moravian Church. Three daughters survived.

1063. **Fredericka Augusta Etschman,** m.n. Venter. xxxi, n. 4. Sept. 22. Daughter of John Henry and Theresa Henrietta (Roeder) Venter. Born in

Lobenstein, Saxony, June 16, 1830. When she was about three years old, her parents emigrated to the United States, settling near Nazareth. Confirmed in Schoeneck. Married Francis Xavier Etschman, in Philadelphia, March 8, 1849. Her husband died in Philadelphia, in 1882; since then she has resided here. Died suddenly, when about to return to Nazareth from Tacony, where she had been visiting her daughter. She was survived by three sons and two daughters.

1064. **Emma Caroline Christina Gramlich,** m.n. Venter. xxxi, n. 5. Oct. 1. (Sister of the preceding one.) Daughter of John Henry and Theresa Henrietta (Roeder) Venter. Born in Lobenstein, Saxony, Dec. 1, 1828. Came with her parents to this country about 1833. Confirmed in the Moravian Church in Bethlehem. Then moved to Philadelphia, and married John Gramlich, March 19, 1849. Moved to Nazareth in 1852. In poor health for some years.

1065. **Mary Ann Sybilla Daniel,** m.n. Schmidt. xxxi, n. 6. Oct. 13. Daughter of John and Sophia (Beck) Schmidt. Born Jan. 10, 1832. Confirmed at Nazareth in 1848. Married James Daniel, March 12, 1854. In 1895, in consequence of poverty and helplessness, she and her husband were removed to the Almshouse, where her husband died, Oct. 9, 1895. The funeral service was held in the chapel of the Almshouse, and interment made in the Nazareth graveyard.

1066. **Rachel Belinda Walter,** m.n. Sellers. xxxi, n. 7. Dec. 16. Daughter of Philip and Hannah (Roberts) Sellers. Born in Germantown, Pa., Feb. 12, 1804. Removed, with her parents, to Whitemarsh, Pa., and there married Dr. Philip Walter, in April, 1823, and then moved to Nazareth. Baptized by Brother Wm. Henry Van Vleck, Oct. 19, 1825. She was very active in the church and served many years as one of the "Saaldienerinnen." Her husband died very suddenly, Dec. 19, 1865. She had nine children, of whom five preceded her into eternity. She had thirteen grand-children and twelve great-grand-children.

1897.

1067. **Franklin Philip Maus.** xxx, s. 17. Died Dec. 31. Buried Jan. 3. Son of John J. and Annie (Heintzelman) Maus. Born April 13, 1896.

1068. **Louisa Cornelia Messinger,** m.n. Wenhold. xxxi, n. 8. Feb. 9. Daughter of Charles and Araminta (Brunner) Wenhold. Born in Schoeneck, June 24, 1842. Confirmed at Nazareth in 1860. Married Aaron Messinger, Sept. 30, 1869. She had three children, all of whom died in infancy.

1069. **James Henry Knapp.** xxxiii, s. 3. May 6. Son of Lebbeus and Elizabeth (Christie) Knapp. Born at Hopewell Centre, near Canandaigua, N.Y., July 29, 1827. From 1861 to 1865 he was clerk in the Patent Office in Washington, D.C. Married Mary J. Daniel, Aug. 9, 1858. She died Sept. 20, 1883. Married Clara A. Christ, Aug. 6, 1885. After the death of Mr. William Christ, they moved to Nazareth. Confirmed at Nazareth, March, 1893. Two daughters, one by the first and one by the second marriage, survived. Died suddenly, aged 69 years.

1070. **Beata Maus.** xxvii, n. 15. May 19. Infant daughter of J. J. and Annie Maus.

1071. **Sarah Louisa Kotz,** m.n. Stoudt. xxxi, n. 9. May 30. Daughter of Jacob and Elizabeth (Kingkinger) Stoudt. Born in Forks Township, Pa., July 2, 1827. Baptized and confirmed in Schoeneck Church. In 1845 united with

Nazareth congregation. Married Charles Kotz, Jan. 5, 1854. He died Oct. 3, 1893.

1072. **Horace Franklin Kingkinger.** xxxiii, s. 4. Oct. 17. Son of Daniel and Rebecca (Cassler) Kingkinger. Born in Bushkill Township, Northampton County, Pa., Oct. 22, 1830. Baptized and confirmed in the Schoeneck Church. Married Mary Eva Schneider, Aug. 22, 1852. In 1858 removed to Nazareth. Served in the 153d Regiment from 1862 to 1863. Re-united with Moravian Church, May, 1877. Served in the Board of Trustees from Dec., 1881 to 1887, being President of the same several years. His wife died Oct. 14, 1888. Two sons and a daughter survived.

1073. **Francis Sylvester Miksch.** xxxiii, s. 5. Oct. 29. Son of Jacob and Catharine (Weinland) Miksch. Born March 9, 1815. A daughter of one of the pioneer settlers from Kunewalde, Moravia. Married Elfrida Danke, March 30, 1837. Served as Trustee, Elder and Representative to two Synods. In 1887 he and his wife celebrated their golden wedding. His married life extended over more than sixty years. He was survived by three children, five grand-children and one great-grand-child.

1074. **Christian Henry Clewell.** xxxiii, s. 6. Nov. 3. Son of Jacob and Rebecca (Seyfried) Clewell. Born June 19, 1826. Married Eliza Peissert of Bethlehem, April 15, 1851. He served as Head Sexton twenty-seven years, as Trustee four years, in the Parochial School Board, in the Public School Board and in the Town Council. As undertaker, he buried 1189 persons. During more than a year he was an invalid. Survived by four children.

1075. **Josephine Kreider,** m.n. Demuth. xxxi, n. 10. Nov. 27. Daughter of William and Maria (Keller) Demuth. Born in Lancaster, April 15, 1831. Married William E. Kreider, Aug. 30, 1855; living in Lititz until 1865, when she moved to Lancaster. Moved to Nazareth in 1890. Her husband died Aug. 29, 1895. She was a devout Christian. Having gone to Lititz to visit her son, the Principal of Linden Hall Seminary, she died there suddenly, of neuralgia of the heart. Two children survived, a daughter, Mrs. George Geiger, of Nazareth, and the Rev. Charles D. Kreider, Principal at Lititz.

1898.

1076. **Robert Irwin Schlabach.** xxxiii, s. 7. Jan. 21. Son of Henry and Lucy (Patterson) Schlabach. Born in Upper Nazareth Township, June 8, 1847. Baptized and confirmed in the Lutheran Church. Married Amelia Matilda Kuntsman. United with the Moravian Church in 1877. He was active in the Sunday-school, being librarian for many years, and also a member of the church choir. From 1883 to 1889 he was a member of the Borough Council; an efficient member of the Board of Trustees of the congregation, and a trustee of Nazareth Hall. He was proprietor of large agricultural implement works; a very progressive man and possessed of more than ordinary ability; a faithful and consistent member of the Church, and greatly respected. During the last years of his life he was a great sufferer.

1077. **Josiah Oliver Beitel.** xxxiii, s. 8. Feb. 6. Son of John and Anna Magdalene (Romig) Beitel. Born in Nazareth, Jan. 23, 1811. He learned the trade of watchmaker with Jedediah Weiss, of Bethlehem, where he married Maria Sophia Kern, Oct. 1, 1833. He was a good musician, a member of the church choir and trombonist. He was a trustee from 1858 to 1860. Also a member of the public school board, and chief burgess during the war. His wife died March 26, 1895. He was survived by five sons, all of whom, with one exception, are watchmakers, the other being a teacher. He had nineteen grand-children and six great-grand-children. In 1883 he and his wife celebrated their golden wedding anniversary. Aged 87 years.

1078. **Elfrida Cornelia Miksch**, m.n. Danke. xxxi, n. 11. May 19. Daughter of John Frederick and Barbara (Ehrenhard) Danke. Born in Nazareth, Feb. 21, 1815. Married Francis Sylvester Miksch, March 30, 1837. In 1887 they observed their golden wedding anniversary. Their married life extended over a period of 60 years and seven months. Her husband died Oct. 29, 1897. She was a very faithful follower of the Saviour. Three children survived, five grand-children and three great-grand-children.

1079. **Augusta Francisca Rosina Schultz**, m.n. Schreiber. xxxi, n. 12. July 6. Daughter of Anton and Rosina Schreiber. Born in Fleckenhost, Westphalia, Germany, March 22, 1818. Baptized and confirmed in the Catholic Church, to which she remained faithful to her end. In June, 1845, came to the United States with a brother, and in August, 1846, married William Schultz, in New York. About forty years she had lived here. She is survived by a daughter.

1080. **Matilda Louisa Kern.** xxxii, n. 1. Sept. 28. Daughter of Andrew G. and Catharine Louisa (Levering) Kern. Born Dec. 7, 1820. Married Peter Kern, Feb. 13, 1845, her married life continuing more than fifty-three years. During several years an invalid.

1081. **Frank James Bardill.** xxxiv, s. 2. Oct. 2. Infant son of John F. and Sevilla (Hoch) Bardill. Born March 2, 1898.

1082. **Beatus Maus.** xxxiv, s. 3. Nov. 17. Infant son of J. J. and Annie Maus.

1083. **John Frederick Warman.** xxxiii, s. 9. Dec. 9. (A former pastor of Nazareth.) Son of Christian L. Arnold and Maria Warman, m.n. Bielitz. Born in Kleinwelka, Saxony, Sept. 23, 1813. Teacher in the Boys' School at Gnadenfeld, from 1832 to 1836, when he was called to Gnadau, where he taught until 1838, when he received a call as missionary to Surinam, S.A. Here he remained three years. Returning, he lived in England, and was "Scripture reader" in Pudsey, near Fulneck. Married Augusta Fredericka Bird, Feb. 3, 1842. Then appointed teacher and assistant to the pastor at Baildon, a village near Fulneck. He had four children, one of whom died in infancy. In 1849 he came to the United States, and for fifteen years was engaged in the Tract Society. In 1864 he was ordained a Deacon, having received a call as missionary among the Indians in Canada. Here his eldest son died. In 1867 called as pastor to Olney, Ill., and ordained a Presbyter. In 1871 appointed as pastor to Nazareth, where he served until 1876. On Aug. 13, 1872, his wife died. Married Angelica W. Reichel, March, 1874. On account of his health, he retired in 1876. In his retirement he was always ready to render what assistance he could to his brethren.

1899.

1084. **Joseph Henry Frack.** xxxiv, s. 4. Jan. 1. Infant son of Edward and Anna (Seyfried) Frack. Born Dec. 10, 1898.

1085. **Charles Edgar Crawford.** xxxi, s. 9. Jan. 5. Son of Dr. W. H. and Julia A. (Mohn) Crawford. Born in Nazareth, July 6, 1879. Died at Elwyn, Pa., aged 19 years.

1086. **Eva Cecilia Jane Neumeyer,** m.n. Bonstein. xxxii, n. 2. May 6. Born July 21, 1860, near Nazareth. Confirmed in the Reformed Church. Married John Maurice Neumeyer, Sept. 25, 1879. United with Moravian Church, April, 1886.

1087. **Richard Benjamin Christ.** xxxiii, s. 10. Aug. 29. Son of John Jacob and Anna Justina (Knauss) Christ. Born in Nazareth, Jan. 16, 1812. Married Fredericka Danke, March 15, 1845. Of his children, only one son survived. His wife died in 1865. Nov. 6, 1865, married Amelia Giersch, who died in 1884. He was not merely a skillful manufacturer of hats, carrying on a large business, but a well-known naturalist, for years associated with the Smithsonian Institute in Washington, and regarded as an authority on many subjects of interest. He was a man of more than ordinary intelligence, a close observer of nature, which led him, reverently and devoutly, to nature's God. He held various offices in the church.

1088. **Susan Adelaide Mack.** xxvii, n. 16. Sept. 6. Daughter of Edw. T. and Mary (Milchsack) Mack. Born Feb. 23, 1889.

1900.

1089. **Alice Hammer Kreider.** xxvii, n. 17. Feb. 17. Infant daughter of the Rev. Charles D. and Emily (Hammer) Kreider. Born at Lititz, April 17, 1899. Died at Lititz.

1090. **John Frederick Carl.** xxxiv, s. 5. Feb. 20. Son of John Carl and Emma Haas. Born in Cleveland, O., Aug. 4, 1892.

1091. **Jacob Matthew Ettwein.** xxxiii, s. 11. March 16. Son of John Ettwein and great-grand-son of Bishop John Ettwein. Born in Georgetown, Lower Nazareth Township, Oct. 18, 1830. Married Sophia Catharine Miksch, daughter of Jacob and Catharine Miksch, April 11, 1854. He had two children, both of whom died in infancy. His wife died Jan. 17, 1892.

1092. **Annabella Knauss,** m.n. Beitel. xxxii, n. 3. March 29. Daughter of John and Anna M. (Romig) Beitel. Born in Nazareth, Sept. 13, 1813. Married George Knauss, July 27, 1845, who died May 14, 1888. Survived by a son, William V. Knauss, of Bethlehem.

1093. **Mary Horner Etschman,** m.n. Blair. xxxii, n. 4. April 19. Daughter of James R. and Martha Wilson Blair. Born near Bath, Pa., April 3, 1854. Baptized in and joined Presbyterian Church. Married Edwin R. Etschman, Sept. 20, 1877, and two years later united with the Moravian Church at Nazareth. Previous to her marriage she had taught the school in the Almshouse, and during the last seventeen years, she and her husband had been stewards at the Hospital of the Alms-house. She was loved by all the inmates, and was very faithful and kind. Died at Kensington Hospital, Philadelphia, where she had undergone an operation. One daughter survived.

1094. **Louis Franklin Memmert.** xxxiv, s. 6. June 14. Son of William and Sarah J. (Werkheiser) Memmert. Born in Nazareth, Sept. 11, 1888.

1095. **Mattie Marguerite Cooley.** xxxiii, n. 2. July 21. Infant daughter of Harry and Clara (Miksch) Cooley. Born in Easton, June 6, 1899.

1096. **Jacob William Culp.** xxxiii, s. 12. July 28. Son of Jacob and Christiana Culp. Born in Philadelphia, May 20, 1841. Married Ellen (Sellers) Culp, June 5, 1871.

1901.

1097. **Agnes Klein,** m.n. Lutz. xxxii, n. 5. Died Dec. 29, 1900. Buried Jan. 2, 1901. Born in Würtemberg, Nov. 13, 1825. Baptized and confirmed in the Reformed Church. After her arrival in this country, married Henry Klein, in New York, May 6, 1855. United with the Moravian Church, in Nazareth, 1860. Her husband died June 13, 1890.

1098. **William McKinley Stark.** xxxiv, s. 7. Jan. 6. Son of Jacob Stark.

1099. **Polly Hinkel.** xxix, n. 7. Jan. 24. Born at Schoeneck, Feb. 29, 1816. Died at Bethlehem, aged 84 years.

1100. **Henry Reese.** xxxiii, s. 13. Feb. 7. Son of Jacob and Leah (George) Reese. Born in Lower Nazareth Township, Nov. 16, 1839. He was a member of the Schoeneck congregation.

1101. **Mary Haehnle.** xxxiii, n. 3. April 2. Infant daughter of the Rev. Charles A. and Alice F. (DeRemer) Haehnle. Born March 31, 1901.

1102. **Anna Matilda Seyfried,** m.n. Kram. xxxii, n. 6. April 1. Daughter of John Kram. Born Nov. 28, 1823. Married Christian Henry Seyfried, in March, 1844, who died June 29, 1860. She had six children, of whom one daughter died in childhood. During more than thirty years was employed in Nazareth Hall as sick-nurse and general assistant. Died at the home of her daughter in Schoeneck.

1103. **Jeremiah Abel.** xxxiii, s. 14. Aug. 8. Son of Rudolph and Susanna (Schaefer) Abel. Born in East Allen Township, July 20, 1858. Baptized and confirmed in the Lutheran Church. Married Mary Ziegler, Oct. 27, 1888, and united with the Moravian Church in 1899. He had two children.

1104. **William Henry Kern.** xxxiii, s. 15. Aug. 13. Son of John and Elizabeth (Stocker) Kern. Born in Niesky, Feb. 17, 1829. Baptized amd confirmed in the Reformed Church. United with the Moravian Church. Married Louisa Ebbecke, Nov. 6, 1851. He had four sons and a daughter, one son dying before the father.

1105. **Edward Lewis Abel.** xxxi, s. 10. Aug. 23. Son of Lewis and Elmira (Clewell) Abel. Born in Nazareth, Sept. 19, 1876. Died in Bethlehem, where his parents reside.

1106. **Jacob Cope.** xxxiii, s. 16. Aug. 31. Son of Ph. and Maria (Miller) Cope. Born in Lower Saucon Township, June 27, 1814. Baptized and confirmed in the Lutheran Church. Married Lavina Adam, Nov. 27, 1844. He had twelve children of whom eight survive. United with the Moravian Church in 1884.

1107. **Martha Grunert,** m.n. Smyth. xxxii, n. 7. Sept. 27. Daughter of John and Anna Benigna (Clarke) Smyth. Born near Philadelphia, May 13, 1824. Baptized Dec. 22, 1839, by Bishop David Bigler in Philadelphia. Entered Bethlehem Seminary as teacher in 1845, continuing there twenty-six years. Married the widower, Rev. Max E. Grunert, Sept. 7, 1871, and, with him, as Principal of Salem Academy, served until 1877, when they were called to Emmaus, and in 1879 to Bethlehem, Brother Grunert being resident professor in the Theological Seminary. In July, 1886, removed to Nazareth, where he died June 4, 1887. She was respected and beloved by all who knew her.

1108. **Emma Aurelia Speer**, m.n. Seyfried. xxxii, n. 8. Sept. 29. Daughter of John and Anna (Eyerly) Seyfried. Born July 23, 1828. Baptized and confirmed in the Moravian Church at Nazareth, but, after her marriage to George F. Speer, she united with the Lutheran Church.

1109. **Carl Monroe Kiefer.** xxxiv, s. 8. Nov. 30. Son of Augustus and Eva (Rice) Kiefer. Born Jan. 22, 1899.

1110. **Jacob Henry Beck.** xxxiii, s. 17. Dec. 22. Son of Jacob F. and Caroline (Stauber) Beck. Born June 26, 1829. Married Lydia Ann Nolf May 27, 1855. Of his five children, two sons survive. He was Justice of the Peace for more than thirty years, and at the time of his death, was treasurer of the congregation. He had been in poor health and a great sufferer for several years.

1902.

1111. **Thomas Seyfried.** xxxi, s. 11. Feb. 23. Son of Philip and Anna Benigna (Gambold) Seyfried. Born in Bushkill Township, July 27, 1825. Died in consequence of an accident.

1112. **Abraham Gruver.** xxxiii, s. 18. March 19. Son of George and Sarah (Hartman) Gruver. Born in Forks Township, July 29, 1838. Married Sarah Eliza Schmidt, March 14, 1858. United with the congregation in 1862. One daughter survived.

1113. **Lydia Pauline Kern,** m.n. Hauser. xxxii, n. 9. April 9. Daughter of Christian and Anna (Spaugh) Hauser. Born at Bethabara, N. C., June 8, 1828. Married James Martin Rominger in 1852. Her husband died from exposure, as a soldier in the Southern army, in 1864. She moved to Bethlehem, Philadelphia, and in 1882 to Nazareth. Of her children, a son and daughter survive. She was sick-nurse at the Hall for some time. Married the widower Gustav A. Kern, Aug. 28, 1890. After great suffering died April 9.

1114. **William Ebner.** xxxv, s. 2. June 1. Son of Conrad and Magdalene (Straub) Ebner. Born in Columbia County, Pa., Sept. 22, 1826. Married Mary Thomas, Feb. 17, 1848, at Bloomsburg, Pa. He had four children, of whom only one, Mrs. Richard Beitel, survives. In 1901 removed to Nazareth, to the home of his daughter. He was a member of the Methodist Episcopal Church.

1115. **Gustav Adolph Kern.** xxxv, s. 3. Aug. 3. Son of Christian and Maria Elizabeth (Bishop) Kern. Born in Bethlehem, April 11, 1817. As a young man moved to Nazareth, carrying on a successful business. Married Julianna Emilie Clewell, m.n. Danke, July 18, 1858. She died Feb. 9, 1877. Married Lydia P. Rominger, Aug. 28, 1890, who died April 9, 1902. He was a very good man, and an excellent member of the Church.

1116. **Jane Kortz,** m.n. Kern. xxxii, n. 10. Oct. 11. Daughter of William and Louisa (Ebbecke) Kern. Born at Niesky, April 29, 1858. Married Edwin S. Kortz, Dec. 6, 1882, and moved to Philadelphia. Husband died May 10, 1893, and she then returned to Nazareth with her two children.

1117. **Ellen Brockmann,** m.n. Wenhold. xxxii, n. 11. Nov. 18. Daughter of Charles and Araminta (Brunner) Wenhold. Born Aug. 30, 1849. She was a very active woman and assisted in the church in various ways. Died in the Easton Hospital, after undergoing an operation. A son survives.

1903.

1118. **Araminta Emilie Boerstler,** m.n. Clewell. xxxii, n. 12. Feb. 16. Daughter of Joseph and Elizabeth Clewell. Born in Nazareth, June 19, 1821. Married James Boerstler. Died in Philadelphia, where she had resided.

1119. **Ellen Araminta Gordon,** m.n. Beidleman. xxxiv, n. 1. March 8. Daughter of George and Elizabeth Beidleman. Born in Bushkill Township, Jan. 9, 1858. Confirmed at Nazareth in 1886. Married Harry Gordon, April 12, 1886. Died at Passaic, N. J.

1120. **Andrew Benjamin Whitesell.** xxxv, s. 4. May 14. Son of Charles and Catharine (Leininger) Whitesell. Born Feb. 2, 1833. Married Mary Ann Loutz, Jan. 21, 1860. Died in Bethlehem, where he had resided for some time.

1121. **Florian Franklin Giering.** xxxv, s. 5. June 16. Son of John and Catharine (Doll) Giering. Born in Emmaus, Feb. 6, 1828. Married Susan Elizabeth Saylor, Feb. 28, 1850. Lived in Catasauqua nineteen years. In 1872 moved to Bethlehem, and to Nazareth in 1875. His wife died Sept. 1, 1894. He had been in poor health for several years.

1122. **Maria Louisa Augusta Schwarze,** m.n. Schroeder. xxxiv, n. 2. June 25. Born in Berlin, Germany, Aug. 11, 1839. Married Herman William Koehler, April 1, 1862. Four children, only one of whom survived. Her husband died Oct. 30, 1883, and she then came to New York, with her son. Married, at Utica, N.Y., the Rev. Ernst Schwarze, at that time pastor in Elizabeth, N.J. Later she served, with him, the congregation in Egg Harbor City, N.J. In 1898 moved to Nazareth. After being in feeble health for some years, died rather unexpectedly.

1123. **Frank Clewell Steckel.** xxxi, s. 12. July 16. Son of William R. and Maria (Clewell) Steckel. Born in Allentown, Jan. 23, 1872. Died in Philadelphia, aged 31 years.

1124. **Morris Dudley Cooley.** xxxiv, s. 9. July 29. Infant son of Harry and Clara (Miksch) Cooley. Born Dec. 12, 1902.

1125. **Peter Kern.** xxxv, s. 6. Aug. 11. Son of John and Elizabeth (Stocker) Kern. Born at Niesky, Jan. 22, 1819. Baptized and confirmed in the Reformed Church. United with the Moravian Church in 1851. Married Matilda Louisa Kern, Feb. 13, 1845. His wife died Sept. 28, 1898. One son survived. For many years he was one of the sacristans (dieners) of the church.

1126. **Marietta Kern,** m.n. Rilbert. xxxiv, n. 3. Aug. 18. Daughter of George and Mary (Smith) Rilbert. Born near Saylorsburg, Sept. 4, 1834. Married William T. Kern, Dec. 29, 1864, who died March 1, 1879.

1127. **Thomas Ely Dereamer.** xxxv, s. 7. Oct. 3. Son of William and Mary Ann (Ely) Dereamer. Born June 18, 1858. Married Antoinette Kirchenthal, Dec. 24, 1884. One son survives. For nearly sixteen years he was a sacristan (diener) of the church.

1128. **Henry Eugene Etschman.** xxxv, s. 8. Dec. 8. Son of Francis and Augusta (Venter) Etschman. Born Oct. 28, 1855. Married, Dec. 30, 1880, Katharine Wolf. A few years ago he returned to Nazareth from Philadelphia, where he had resided.

1904.

1129. **Augusta Seyfried.** xxix, n. 8. Jan. 2. Daughter of Philip and Anna Benigna (Gambold) Seyfried. Born in Bushkill Township, July 28, 1823.

1130. **William Henry Clewell.** xxxv, s. 9. Jan. 27. Son of Thomas and Florentine (Leibert) Clewell. Born in Nazareth, May 1, 1845. He served in the war, in the 153d Pennsylvania Regiment. Married Catharine Trein, Oct. 18, 1877. Died at Rittersville.

1131. **Louisa Magdalene Ritter,** m.n. Culver. xxxiv, n. 4. March 20. Born near Nazareth, Nov. 23, 1842. Married John Henry Ritter, who died Sept. 19, 1895. One son survived her.

1132. **Maria Kiefer,** m.n. Heller. xxxiv, n. 5. April 2. Daughter of John Heller. Born March 16, 1849. Married Mr. Gross, this union being blessed with a son and a daughter. Married William R. Kiefer, Sept. 14, 1865.

1133. **Harriet Eliza Leibfried,** m.n. Beitel. xxxiv, n. 6. April 10. Daughter of Christian Henry Beitel. Born July 19, 1813. Married John C. Leibfried, April 27, 1834, who died January 31, 1880. Two daughters and a son survive her. She had eleven grand-children, thirteen great-grand-children, and one great-great-grand-child.

1134. **Charles Edward Michael.** xxxiv, s. 10. May 26. Infant son of C. William and Ida (Silfies) Michael.

1135. **Charles Edwin Venter.** xxxi, s. 13. June 19. Only son of Emanuel and Cornelia (Cope) Venter. Born May 24, 1874. He was active in the Sunday-school and Christian Endeavor Society and Church. A faithful young man.

	XXXV
1130 1128 1129 1125 1121 1120 1115 1114	XXXV
1134 1124 1109 1098 1094 1090 1084 1082 1081	XXXIV
1112 1110 1106 1104 1103 1100 1096 1091 1087 1083 1077 1076 1074 1073 1072 1069 1057	XXXIII

1053 1052 1051 1050 1048 1044 1042 1033 1031 1030 1024 1022 1001 998 997 995 991 989	XXX
1123 1111 1105 1085 1068 1056 1055 1049 1040 1027 1045 988	XXIX
1067 1059 1013 1016 1008 1007 1004 999 996 987 978 977 975 974 970 964 952	XXVIII
985 984 983 980 979 976 971 967 962 961 946 944 943 938 933 931 930 926	XXVII
924 920 919 915 912 905 903 897 895 885 882 881 880 877 872 867 862 856	XXVI
947 936 922 925 916 898 889 883 869 864 863 859 855 843 842 839 833 832	XXV
849 845 838 837 835 828 827 824 820 818 816 811 808 802 800 785 778 777	XXIV
830 822 812 810 809 801 795 791 784 780 773 769 768 766 764 757 756	XX
914 909 892 873 871 870 866 836 829 817 796 793 772 762 761 759 752 736	XXII
776 774 771 770 763 748 743 742 741 718 716 714 709 704 702 699 697 696	XXI

South

686 688 692 700 701 703 705 715 720 722 724 725 726 728 729 731 732 737	XXI
683 681 673 677 667 661 655 646 644 643 642 638 636 631 630 629 627 626	XXI
694 693 691 690 684 673 671 668 664 654 652 650 635 620 616 599 573 589	XX
568 572 574 575 579 580 584 585 591 596 598 600 606 610 612 617 618 623	XIX
621 595 592 582 577 576 569 565 561 558 555 553 537 535 533 521 510 507	XVII
552 550 547 546 541 540 538 531 530 528 525 523 519 514 512 511 506 505	XVI
504 495 492 484 482 481 480 470 468 462 460 459 452 450 447 438 433 431	XVIII
430 428 422 414 411 410 408 407 405 400 391 389 388 383 381 378 372 369	XV
361 360 359 352 349 347 335 334 328 326 318 313 304 302 297 275 283 260	XIV
333 315 312 311 307 305 291 279 277 272 264 252 244 241 238 227 223 222	XIII
296 289 285 282 276 268 267 263 262 258 255 254 248 247 246 245 235 233	XII
280 232 225 224 215 211 210 209 208 205 193 191 173 166 165 163 162 152	XI
500 499 494 490 488 487 478 476 469 466 455 449 445 443 437 432 427 421	X
154 148 143 141 135 129 127 118 106 90 43 31 28 27 16 12 7 1	IX
160 156 139 137 131 128 126 119 115 105 88 84 73 69 68 64 63 53	VIII
269 261 231 230 229 228 226 213 85 86 39 38 37 36 35 34 30 25	VII
271 270 257 253 251 216 219 162 99 98 23 20 19 18 16 10 8 5	VI
419 412 403 402 397 390 380 344 339 336 322 319 317 316 298 293 292 281	V
202 198 197 192 190 177 172 145 100 98 55 52 47 45 44 42 41 40	IV
237 266 195 189 183 170 142 133 109 96 83 82 74 72 70 60 59 58	III
213 217 241 200 187 153 151 132 117 116 76 67 50 33 26 22 11 9	II
204 186 158 150 194 136 134 123 122 120 114 112 110 108 92 80 79 77	I

1129 1122 1126 1131 1132 1133
1095 1101

1080 1086 1092 1093 1097 1102 1107 1108 1113 1116 1117 1118
1060 1061 1062 1063 1064 1065 1066 1068 1071 1075 1078 1079
1022 1028 1029 1034 1035 1038 1039 1041 1043 1045 1046 1047
958 963 970 1010 1026 1037 1099 1129
966 969 973 982 792 993 1002 1003 1009 1011 1012 1013 1014 1017 1019 1020 1021
917 959 963 972 981 986 994 1000 1005 1006 1025 1032 1036 1054 1070 1088 1089
907 908 910 917 918 921 923 911 934 937 939 940 941 950 955 956 960
850 851 853 854 857 861 865 868 876 878 884 890 896 900 902 904 906
833 790 798 815 841 846 882 875 879 887 894 901 913 928 935 948 947
777 781 787 788 792 794 797 803 805 813 814 819 823 831 840 844 848

North

---

447 858 860 721 874 886 888 891 893 899 922 927 929 942 948 951 953 954
651 653 656 657 660 663 666 669 672 676 682 685 689 695 698 707 708 711
633 734 735 728 747 755 767 782 786 789 799 804 806 807 821 825 826 834
70 680 717 727 730 734 740 744 745 746 749 750 751 753 754 758 760 765 775
625 640 641 645 648 657 658 662 665 674 678 679 687 706 710 712 719 722

556 578 581 586 588 594 605 607 608 609 613 614 616 618 632 634 647 649
60 561 563 567 578 573 587 590 597 601 602 611 619 622 624 633 637 639
65 324 353 377 385 392 398 404 406 409 415 418 425 442 444 451 453 534
16 420 426 429 435 436 440 441 448 461 463 482 485 491 493 503 513 520
63 364 366 370 373 374 375 376 382 384 387 392 394 395 396 401 516 543
74 269 256 259 274 275 286 287 290 294 299 300 301 327 329 330 518 545
65 471 472 475 479 486 496 502 508 509 517 529 544 553 603 644 713 965
48 51 54 57 61 62 65 71 138 164 178 180 314 338 357 358 522 551
6 13 14 17 21 29 32 46 171 179 182 219 321 340 351 356 532 554
75 78 87 89 91 97 104 107 175 194 202 221 309 341 350 354 549 557
11 124 140 155 161 167 168 169 181 196 212 234 303 342 343 348 542 564
78 284 306 308 323 332 337 345 355 454 456 458 464 515 517 524 545 549
2 3 4 24 47 56 66 81 199 206 236 240 498 497 501 516 536 556
01 113 130 146 149 159 184 185 188 207 289 293 467 473 474 477 489 559
93 74 103 121 125 147 157 176 220 241 250 273 399 413 423 424 437 571
88 310 320 325 331 346 362 365 367 368 371 379 386 417 434 439 446

INDEX

TO THE

MORAVIAN CEMETERIES

OF

NAZARETH.

Metalmark Books is a joint imprint of The Pennsylvania State University
Press and the Office of Digital Scholarly Publishing at The Pennsylvania State University Libraries. The facsimile editions published under this
imprint are reproductions of out-of-print, public domain works that hold
a significant place in Pennsylvania's rich literary and cultural past.
Metalmark editions are primarily reproduced from the University Libraries' extensive
Pennsylvania collections and in cooperation with other
state libraries. These volumes are available to the public for viewing online
and can be ordered as print-on-demand paperbacks.

LIBRARY OF CONGRESS CATALOGING-IN-PUBLICATION DATA

Kluge, Edward T., 1831–1912.
The Moravian graveyards at Nazareth, Pa., 1744–1904 / Edward T. Kluge.
p.   cm.
"Metalmark Books."
Summary: "A listing of burials in various Moravian cemeteries in Nazareth, Pennsylvania. Originally published in 1906"—Provided by publisher.
Includes bibliographical references and index.
ISBN 978-0-271-06036-1 (pbk. : alk. paper)
1. Cemeteries—Pennsylvania—Nazareth.
2. Registers of births, etc.—Pennsylvania—Nazareth.
3. Moravians—Pennsylvania—Nazareth—Genealogy.
4. Nazareth (Pa.)—Genealogy.
I. Title.

F159.N3K55 2013
929.3748'22—dc23
2012043857

Printed in the United States of America
Reprinted by The Pennsylvania State University Press, 2012
University Park, PA 16802-1003